BORROWED FINERY

ALSO BY PAULA FOX

Novels

Poor George
Desperate Characters
The Western Coast
The Widow's Children
A Servant's Tale
The God of Nightmares

Books for Children

Maurice's Room
A Likely Place
How Many Miles to Babylon?
The Stone-faced Boy
Good Ethan
Hungry Fred
Dear Prosper
Portrait of Ivan
Blowfish Live in the Sea
The Slave Dancer
A Place Apart
One-eyed Cat
The Moonlight Man
Lily and the Lost Boy
The Village by the Sea
Monkey Island
Amzat and his Brothers
The Little Swineherd and Other Tales
Western Wind
The Eagle Kite
Radiance Descending

BORROWED FINERY

a memoir

Paula Fox

TED SMART

This edition produced for The Book People Ltd,
Hall Wood Avenue, Haydock, St Helens WA11 9UL

Flamingo
An Imprint of HarperCollins*Publishers*
77–85 Fulham Palace Road,
Hammersmith, London W6 8JB

www.**fireandwater**.com

Flamingo is a registered trademark of
HarperCollins*Publishers* Limited.

Published by Flamingo 2002
1 3 5 7 9 8 6 4 2

First published in the USA by
Henry Holt and Co. 2001

Portions of this book appeared in *Pequod, Triquarterly, Threepenny Review*, and *The Pushcart Prize XXIV*

A catalogue record for this book
is available from the British Library

ISBN 0 00 767343 4

Set in Horley Old Style MT by
Rowland Phototypesetting Ltd, Bury St Edmunds, Suffolk

Printed and bound in Great Britain by
William Clowes Limited, Beccles and London

For my family, my husband, Martin Greenberg,
and for Sheila Gordon,
who sustained me throughout this work
with her endless patience and affection

"After so long grief, such nativity!"

—*The Comedy of Errors*

BORROWED FINERY

When I was seventeen, I found a job in what was then downtown Los Angeles in a store where dresses were sold for a dollar each. The store survived through its monthly going-out-of-business sales.

Every few days I was required to descend to the basement to bring up fresh stock to replace what had been sold. It was a vast space, barely lit by a weak bulb hanging from a low ceiling, and appeared to extend beyond the boundaries of the store itself. In its damp reaches I sometimes glimpsed a rat shuttling along a pipe, its naked tail like an earthworm.

Against one wall, piled up on roughly carpentered wood shelves, were flimsy boxes of dresses. In front of the opposite wall was an enormous cardboard cutout, at least ten feet high, of Santa Claus, his sled, and his reindeer. I guessed this was displayed in the store upstairs at Christmastime.

One morning when I was sent to the basement for dresses, I noticed drops of sweat on Santa's brow. Later it occurred to me that the pipe along which I'd seen rats running extended over the cutout, and leaks could account for the appearance of sweat. But at the time I imagined it was because of his outfit. He was as inappropriately dressed for the California climate as I was in my thick blue tweed suit.

I've long forgotten who gave the suit to me. I do recall it was a couple of sizes too big and sewn of such grimly durable wool that the jacket and skirt could have stood upright on the floor.

I earned scant pay at a number of jobs I found and lost that year, barely enough for rent and food with nothing to spare for clothes. What I owned in the way of a wardrobe could have fitted into the sort of suitcase now referred to in luggage ads as a "weekender," a few scraps that would cover me but wouldn't serve in extremes of weather—and, of course, the blue tweed suit that I wore to work in the Los Angeles dress store day after day.

In that time I understood mouse money but not cat money. Five dollars were real. I could stretch them so they would last. I was bewildered even by the thought of fifty dollars. How much was $50?

The actress ZaSu Pitts, in a publicity still—an advertisement for the movie *Greed* made in 1923, the year I was born, that showed her crouching half naked among heaps of gold coins, an expression of demented rapacity on her face—embodied my view of American capitalism when I was a young girl. As I grew older, my attitude about money changed. I began to see how complex it was, how some people accumulate it for its own sake, driven by forces as mysterious to me as those that drive termites to build mounds that attain heights of as much as forty feet in certain parts of the world.

At the same time that I began to acquire material things, my appetite for them was aroused. Yet in my mind's eye, the image of ZaSu Pitts holding out handfuls of gold coins, not offering them but gloating over her possession of them, persists, an image both condemnatory and triumphant.

Balmville

The Reverend Elwood Amos Corning, the Congregational minister who took care of me in my infancy and earliest years and whom I called Uncle Elwood, always saw to it that I didn't look down and out. Twice a year, in the spring and fall, he bought a few things for me to wear, spending what he could from the yearly salary paid to him by his church. Other clothes came my way donated by the mothers in his congregation whose own children had outgrown them. They were mended, washed, and ironed before they were handed on.

In early April, before my fifth birthday, my father mailed Uncle Elwood two five-dollar bills and a written note. I can see him reading the note as he holds it and the bills in one hand, while with the index finger of the other he presses the bridge of his eyeglasses against his nose because he has broken the sidepiece. This particularity of memory can be partly attributed to the rarity of my father's notes—not to mention enclosures of money—or else to the new dress that part of the ten dollars paid for. Or so I imagine.

The next morning Uncle Elwood drove me in his old Packard from the Victorian house on the hill in Balmville, New York, where we lived, to Newburgh, a valley town half an hour distant and a dozen miles north of the Storm King promontory, which sinks into the Hudson River like an elephant's brow.

We parked on Water Street in front of a barbershop where I was taken at intervals to have my hair cut. One morning after we had left the shop, and because I was lost in reverie, staring down at the sidewalk but not seeing it, I reached up to take Uncle Elwood's hand and walked nearly a block before I realized I was holding the hand of a stranger. I let go and turned around and saw that everyone who was on the street was waiting to see how far I would go and what I would do when I looked up. Watching were both barbers from their shop doorway, Uncle Elwood with his hands clasped in front of him, three or four people on their way somewhere, and the stranger whose hand I had been holding. They were all smiling in anticipation of my surprise. For a moment the street was transformed into a familiar room in a beloved house. Still, I was faintly alarmed and ran back to Uncle Elwood.

Our destination that day was Schoonmaker's department store, next to the barbershop. When we emerged back on the sidewalk, he was carrying a box that contained a white dotted-swiss dress. It had a Peter Pan collar and fell straight to its hem from a smocked yoke.

Uncle Elwood had written a poem for me to recite at

the Easter service in the church where he preached. Now I would have something new to wear, something in which I could stand before the congregation and speak his words. I loved him, and I loved the dotted-swiss dress.

Years later, when I read through the few letters and notes my father had written to Uncle Elwood, and which he had saved, I realized how Daddy had played the coquette in his apologies for his remissness in supporting me. His excuses were made with a kind of fraudulent heartiness, as though he were boasting, not confessing. His handwriting, though, was beautiful, an orderly flight of birds across the yellowing pages.

Uncle Elwood made parish visits most Sundays in Washingtonville, at that time still small enough to be called a village, in Orange County, New York, seventeen miles from Balmville, where most members of his congregation lived. The church where he preached was in Blooming Grove, a hamlet a mile or so west of Washingtonville, on a high ridge above a narrow country lane, and so towering—it appeared to me—it could have been a massive white ship anchored there, except for its steeple, which rose toward the heavens like prayerful hands, palms pressed together.

Behind it stood an empty manse and, farther away, a small cemetery. To the right of the church portal was a partly collapsed stable with dark cobwebbed stalls, one of which was still used by a single parishioner, ancient bearded Mr. Howell, who drove his buckboard and horse up the gravel-covered road that led to the church. He always arrived a minute or two before Sunday service began, dressed in a threadbare black overcoat in all seasons of the year, its collar held tight to his throat by a big safety pin. He seemed to me that rock of ages we sang about in the hymn.

After the service, we sometimes called upon two women, an elderly woman and her unmarried daughter, who looked as old as her mother, both in the church choir, whose thin soprano quavers continued long past the moment when other choir members had ceased to sing and had resumed their seats. They appeared not to notice they were the only people still standing in the choir stall.

They lived in a narrow wooden two-story house that resembled most of the other houses in Washingtonville. They would give us Sunday dinner in a back room that ran the width of the house and could accommodate a table large enough for the four of us. It was a distance from the kitchen, where they usually ate their meals, and there was much to-ing and fro-ing as they brought dishes and took them away, adding, it felt to me, years of waiting to the minutes when we actually ate. Summer heat bore down on that back room. It was stifling, hot as burning kindling under the noonday sun. Everything flashed and glittered—cutlery, water glasses, window panes—and drained the food of color.

When we visited Emma Board and her family in another part of the village, I felt a kind of happiness and, at the same time, an apprehension—like that of a traveler who returns to a country where she has endured inexplicable suffering.

I had arrived at the Boards' house when I was two months old, brought there by Katherine, the eldest of four Board children. She had taken me to Virginia on her brief honeymoon with Russell, her new husband. When they returned, her mother was sufficiently recovered from Spanish influenza to take care of an infant.

I heard the tale decades later from Brewster, one of Katherine's two brothers, who had lived in New York City with Leopold, one of my mother's four brothers. I had been left in a Manhattan foundling home a few days after my birth by my reluctant father, and by Elsie, my mother, panic-stricken and ungovernable in her haste to have done with me.

My grandmother, Candelaria, during a brief visit to New York City from Cuba, where she lived on a sugar plantation most of the year, inquired of Leopold the whereabouts of his sister and the baby she knew had been born a few weeks earlier. He said he didn't know where my parents had gone, but that over his objections they had placed me in a foundling home before leaving town—if indeed they had left.

When she heard where I was, my grandmother went at once to the home and took me away. But what could she do with me? She was obliged to return to Cuba within days. For a small monthly stipend, she served as companion to a rich old cousin, the plantation owner, who was subject to fits of lunacy.

It was Brewster who suggested she hand me over to Katherine, who carried me in her arms on her bridal journey to Norfolk.

By chance, by good fortune, I had landed in the hands of rescuers, a fire brigade that passed me along from person to person until I was safe. When we visited the old woman and her daughter, or any other of the minister's parishioners, I was diffident and self-conscious for the first few minutes. But not ever at the Boards'.

For a very short period of my infancy, I had belonged in that house with that family. At some moment during our visits there, I would go down the cellar steps and see if a brown rattan baby buggy and a creaking old crib, used at one time or another by all the Board children and for three months by me, were still stored there. I think the family kept them so I would always find them.

I was five months old when the minister, hearing of my presence in Washingtonville and the singular way I had arrived, an event that had ruffled the nearly motionless, pond-like surface of village life—and knowing the uncertainty of my future, for the Boards, like most of their neighbors in those years, were poor—came by one Sunday to look at me. I was awake in the crib. I might have smiled up at him. In any event, I aroused his interest and compassion. He offered to take me, and, partly due to their straitened circumstances, the Boards agreed to let me go.

* * *

After he finished his sermon, Uncle Elwood would step aside from the pulpit. As the choir rose to sing, he would clasp his hands and gaze down at me where I sat alone in a front pew. There would be the barest suggestion of a smile on his face, a lightening of his Sunday look of solemnity.

The intimacy of those moments between us would give way when a church deacon passed a collection plate among the congregation, now hushed by an upwelling sense of the sacred that followed a reading of Bible verse. When he reached my pew, I would drop in a coin given me earlier by Uncle Elwood.

Later, when I stood beside him at the church portal while people filed out and shook his hand, and old Mr. Howell hurried by, mumbling his thanks for the sermon in a rusty, hollow voice, the feeling of intimacy returned.

I was known to the congregation as the minister's little girl, and thinking of that, I was always gladdened. I turned to him after Mr. Howell had vanished into the stable, noting as I usually did the formality of his preaching clothes, the pearl stickpin in his black and silver tie, a silken stripe running down the side of the black trousers, the beetle-winged tails of his black jacket.

It was like the Sunday a week earlier, and all the Sundays I could recall. I slipped my hand into his, and he clasped it firmly. I watched Mr. Howell, who had backed his buckboard and horse out of the stable and was starting down the road.

My unquestioning trust in Uncle Elwood's love, and in the refuge he had provided for me in the years since Katherine had taken me to her mother, would abruptly collapse. In an instant, I realized the precariousness of my circumstances. I felt the earth crumble beneath my feet. I tottered on the edge of an abyss. If I fell, I knew I would fall forever.

That happened too every Sunday after church. But it lasted no longer than it takes to describe it.

Great storms swept down the Hudson Valley in the summer, especially in August. Thunder and lightning boomed and crackled. The world around the house in Balmville flashed with gusts of wind-driven rain. Through black dissolving windows, trees swayed and bent as they appeared to move closer, to form a circle of leaves and agitated branches that threatened to swallow up the house and us with it.

When the storms struck late at night, Uncle Elwood first woke me—if thunder hadn't already—and then went to his mother's room. He lifted her up from her bed and carried her past the large pier glass at the top of the stairs, and together we went down to the central hall, where he settled her in an armchair he would have moved from the living room earlier that day when he had first noticed black clouds forming in the sky.

Emily Corning had been crippled with arthritis for eighteen years, and she bore the pain of it with patience and austerity as though it were a hard task imposed on her to test her faith inthe deity.

In the flickering yellow glow of the kerosene lamp the minister kept for such emergencies—the electricity always failed during storms—I would stare at the old woman sitting in the shadowed corner, not quite covered by a shawl her son had wrapped around her. A mild smile would touch her colorless lips when she grew aware of my scrutiny. She was unable to lift her head upright and peered at everyone from beneath her brow. She rarely spoke to me, yet I could feel kindness emanating from her just as I could feel the distant warmth of the sun in winter. Her words were few and nearly always about the view of the Hudson River, which she could see from her wheelchair, placed by the minister in front of the three-windowed bay in her bedroom all the mornings that I lived in that house.

Often at night, rarely during the day, and only when she was in terrible pain, I could hear through the closed doors between our bedrooms her gasps for breath, her faint cries, and Uncle Elwood's efforts to comfort her. I would lie rigidly beneath the rose-colored blanket in my bed, imploring God to end what seemed endless, to let her fall asleep.

Sometimes when the thunder had diminished and only rumbled distantly, the minister would light a candle and carry his mother into the living room so she could see the dark wallpaper with its pattern of pussy-willow branches in bloom. She had chosen it decades earlier, when her husband was still living and she had been able to move freely about the house.

At an unexpected clap of thunder nearby, he would bring her back into the hall and return her to her chair, settling her into it as if she were a doll.

He told me with a humorous emphasis in his voice, so I would know not to believe him, that Henry Hudson and his crew were bowling somewhere up the river. But I half believed it.

When the minister's only sister was visiting, and a fierce storm rumbled down the river and blew out the lights, she too sat with us in the downstairs hall, crocheting by lamplight, her face with its pouchy cheeks bent over her work. She asked me to call her "Auntie," which I did as seldom as possible.

As the pealing of the thunder weakened, the old woman and her daughter dozed. Their faces in repose looked sad, as if they had fallen asleep worn out by mourning a loss. Perhaps it was only a trick of the shadows.

I fell asleep too. Uncle Elwood carried me to my bedroom. As he drew up the blanket to cover me, I awoke and saw through my window the lights of Mattewan, a madhouse across the river, glittering among the leaves and branches that struck the panes fiercely as the wind blew.

Auntie had a married daughter who lived in Massachusetts. As far as I knew, she divided her time between that household and ours.

In winter, she regretted ceaselessly and aloud that the heat of the furnace, sent up through dusty registers in the floors of the living room and dining room, didn't reach the bedrooms; in summer, that I made such a dreadful racket running up and down the stairs on my way in or out of the house it gave her headaches—why wasn't there a rug to cover the landing?—and that the meals her brother fixed were skimpy and lacked variety—couldn't he hire a woman on a regular basis to cook and clean, instead of the patchy arrangements with Mrs. So-and-So down the road?

She complained to her brother, when I was within hearing distance, that he gave too much time to certain parishioners of his church—whose services she attended rigorously, a baleful presence among the congregation.

Her voice was often shattered by fits of coughing. She smoked cigarettes, somewhat furtively, and carried a pack of them in a cloth bag, along with scraps of cotton or wool with which she rapidly crocheted small rugs and blankets in colors that suggested mud or blood or urine.

The cloth bag had a wooden handle and was embroidered with a design that made me uneasy. Perhaps it was the reddish entwined loops that led me to think of the copperhead snakes Uncle Elwood had warned me about, lurking in the woods in spring.

Auntie spent most afternoons murmuring to her mother, leaning over in a chair drawn so close to the wheelchair I thought she might topple over. She appeared to be about to creep into the old woman's lap.

But the way she sat was not a posture of intimacy, I think now, or of childlike dependence. Even then I sensed there was resentment in the way she thrust her body at her mother, as though the older woman were still responsible for its miseries.

Could she be telling the story of her divorce over and over again? Uncle Elwood said that she and her husband no longer lived together. They had been divorced. Such an event had never before occurred in the family.

He looked startled as he spoke of it, as though the news had just reached him, although by the time he told me about it, it was old news. Could you escape from a divorce the way you could from a marriage? Was it possible to get a divorce from a divorce?

When the old woman's windows were open and a breeze blew through the room, it wafted Auntie's particular odor toward the doorway where I had paused on my way somewhere—a disagreeable smell composed of tobacco, mothballs, and the cough drops she sucked between cigarettes.

If she wasn't crocheting or whispering to her mother, she followed me about the house, wheedling and hectoring by turns. She was the peevish serpent in the short-lived Eden of my childhood.

There was a three-legged stool in old Mrs. Corning's bedroom that I sometimes moved from its usual place in a corner to her wheelchair and sat on, close to her motionless legs.

Earlier in the day, the minister would have lifted her to a sitting position on the edge of her bed, carried her to the bathroom, placed her on the toilet, waited outside the door until she signaled she was through, brought her back to her room, dressed her in one of her three or four print dresses, and carried her to the wheelchair in front of the bay windows, where she would spend the day until early evening, when he would carry her back to her bed.

She wore soft wool slippers.

She was as unmoving as a woman in a painting. When the day was fine, the sky unclouded, one of those blue American days full of buoyancy and promise that seemed to occur only when I was small, she might break the tranquil silence between us with a remark about the river. How beautiful it always was, she might comment, in her rather toneless voice. She could see Polpis Island and glimpse a bit of West Point just beyond the Storm King mountain. Then she would slip back into silence as though resuming a dream.

Uncle Elwood told me she had been a widow for many years. The dream might have been about her husband, how she had stood with him on the deck of a steamboat, northbound on the Hudson River, and he had seen the land that he would purchase months later to build a house on for her, this very house where she still lived, an old woman confined by illness to a wheelchair.

I looked at her hands, which lay on the wood tray fitted between the chair's arms. They were so twisted they looked like small knobbed claws pointing at each other.

Very slowly, she bowed her head even farther down and smiled at me. It was an impersonal smile, as if pain had worn away any distinctive traits that might have defined her nature.

As I looked up at the slight widening of her mouth, I imagined I recognized a kind of incorporeal kindness—and I think for those few minutes she was able to stand apart from her wounded body.

I couldn't conceive of Uncle Elwood's struggle to make do with the yearly salary he was paid by the church so that it would take care of his mother, himself, and me, along with paying for repairs to the ailing house, any more than I could have conceived of the lives of my parents unfolding somewhere in the world. And I would not have known how poor the Blooming Grove parishioners were, how they could barely afford a pastor of their own.

Behind his mother's closed door, I could hear him telling her, in a voice made loud and incautious by desperation, that he had to replace the coal furnace—which he had to stoke every evening and morning when the weather turned cold—with an oil burner and that the house required a new roof. It leaked so shockingly, he said, he could fly to Jericho!

At his words, *fly to Jericho*, my heart jumped into my throat. It was the most extreme thing I ever heard him utter. He was at the end of his rope! It was the absolute limit!

His protests never lasted more than a few minutes, but the pictures that formed in my mind, evoked by the distress I heard in his voice—usually so serene, so playful—frightened me.

The malevolent furnace, as it labored at night with great

clankings, would climb the stairs and kill us with fire, and the holes in the roof would be enlarged so drastically we would be exposed to the merciless night sky and its rain and wind and cold.

But more terrible by far was the well in the middle of the meadow.

When the water pressure in the house was so low that only a puff of stale air came from the kitchen faucet when it was turned on, and the toilet in the bathroom wouldn't flush, Uncle Elwood set out for the well, carrying a bucket.

I watched in dread from the living room window as he lowered the bucket by a rope tied to his hand. He leaned far out over the edge of the well—too far!—to keep the rope straight as it dropped an instant later, to hit the water with a *plonk*.

He would fall! An enormous jet of well water would lift his drowned body toward the sky, then flood the whole earth!

He hauled on the rope, hand over hand, and at last pulled out the bucket, filled. When I ran out of the house and down the three broad steps of the porch to meet him, he was surprised at the intensity of my relief, as though he had returned safely from a long perilous journey.

Then he recalled what I had told him of my fear when he went to the well. He spoke reassuringly to me, as he did when I was ill. He told me what a fine artesian well it was, how milk snakes kept the water pure. Oh, snakes! Worse!

With his unengaged arm, he clasped me to his side as we walked across the hummocky ground. I was not able to explain to him the extremity of my terror. I couldn't explain it to myself.

Time was long in those days, without measure. I marched through the mornings as if there were nothing behind me or in front of me, and all I carried, lightly, was the present, a moment without end.

From the living room there were views east and south. A line of maple trees and birches marked the southern boundary of the property, and beyond it stood an abandoned mansion. I had walked along its narrow porch among six towering columns and peered through dusty windows at its empty rooms. The ground sloped gently down to the river less than a mile away. It was the same long slope upon which our house stood.

From the windows that faced east, beyond the line of tall sumacs, rose a monastery whose roofs and towers I could see in late autumn and winter, when the deciduous trees surrounding it shed their leaves. At intervals during the day the monastery bells pealed.

When I sat on the porch in my wicker rocking chair in the twilight of a summer's day, eating a supper of cold cereal and buttered bread, I would echo the sounds the bells made by tapping my spoon against the side of the china bowl that had held the cereal. I was alone with my thoughts. They drifted through my mind like clouds that change their shapes as you gaze up at them.

To the north where the storms came from, I could view from the windows in the minister's study a line of tall, thick-trunked evergreen trees and, as though I were on a moving train, catch glimpses of a crumbling wall and some of its fallen stones lying on the pine-needle–strewn ground. Uncle Elwood said the wall had been there when his father bought the property.

Beyond the lawn, which he tended now and then, doggedly and with an air of restrained impatience, pushing a lawn mower with rusty blades, were meadows grown wild. Once or twice a year, a farmer driving a tractor, his wife and their children in a small ramshackle truck behind him, arrived to cut the tall grass and carry it away.

Once the children brought along a sickly puppy and showed it to me. We passed its limp body among us, caressed it, and at last killed it with love. We stared, stricken, at the tiny dog lying dead in the older boy's hands, saliva foaming and dripping from its muzzle. The younger brother began to grin uneasily.

Later that day, after the farmer and his family had departed, I told the minister I had had a hand in the death of the little animal. Although he tried to comfort me, to give me some sort of absolution, I couldn't accept it for many years.

Even now, I am haunted from time to time by the image of

a small group of children, myself among them, standing silently at the back door of the house, looking down at the corpse.

Every spring, thawing snow and rain washed away soil from the surface of the long driveway, leaving deep muddy furrows and exposed stones. I spent hours cracking the stones open, using one for an anvil, another for a hammer, to find out what was inside them. Most appeared to be composed of the same gray matter, but a few revealed streaks of color and different textures in their depths or glinted with sparks of light.

I saw how Uncle Elwood struggled to hold the steering wheel of the car steady as it heaved and skidded along the rough, wet, torn-up ground. But I thought too of how gratifying it was when I found a stone that stood out from the rest because of what was inside it.

The driveway led up to scraggly, patchy lawn, circled the house, then branched off, ending several feet from the entrance to a cave-like, half-collapsed stable that had been built into the side of the slope. Earth nearly covered its roof.

During storms, the minister would race out to the car and drive it into the stable as far as it would go. Once a horse named Dandy Boy had lived in its one stall.

The minister told me stories that illustrated Dandy Boy's high spirits and animal nobility. "He had moxie," he said, and imitated a horse, galloping from the living room where I stood entranced, laughing, into the dining room just as Dandy Boy had galloped into the world.

A while later he took me to a Newburgh soda fountain and ordered a glass of Moxie for me. It had a spiky, electric taste. I imagined Dandy Boy drinking pailfuls of it and afterward rearing up like a cowboy's horse.

In those days there were two movie theaters in Newburgh. Uncle Elwood only took me to movies he had seen, to make sure there was nothing alarming in them. My knowledge of cowboys was limited. But I had seen a Western in which they figured. I was struck by how they clung with their knees to the saddle when their horses circled in one spot and raised up on their hind legs, pawing the air with their hooves as they did in illustrations of books about knights and kings and queens.

When Uncle Elwood returned from evening church functions, he parked the car on a gravel-covered stretch of the driveway next to the house. Nearby stood a few crab-apple trees, neglected but still bearing wizened fruit in autumn. Every autumn she spent with us, Auntie promised to make crab-apple jelly, but she never did.

On those church nights after I was sent to bed by Auntie, or by a neighbor who had come to the house to watch over Uncle Elwood's mother and me, I could never fall asleep, even though my eyelids were often as heavy as stones. I listened, it seemed, with my whole self for the sound of tires rolling on gravel, then halting, then the growl of the engine as it was turned off, a minute of silence, a car door opening and shutting, and not a minute later Uncle Elwood's footsteps on the stairs.

If he came home before dark, I ran to greet him at the front door. If he walked in looking pleased with himself because he had a secret, I would search through his pockets until I found a white paper sack filled with the chocolates he had stopped to buy on his way through Newburgh, and that he and I loved.

One evening he returned from church early. I was still up. There were seven cakes on the back seat of the Packard, each one different, and all made for his birthday by women in the Ladies' Aid Society of the church.

"How shall we ever eat them, Pauli?" he wondered in the hall, looking at the cakes lined up on a table. One by one, I thought to myself.

In late spring, you pluck a blade of tall grass, place it between your thumbs, align it, and blow. The sound you produce is unmelodious, excruciating—and triumphant.

Four bedrooms on the second floor were grouped about the hall landing. There was a bathroom, and a small study with two windows and a narrow door leading out to a balcony that arching, leaf-heavy branches kept cool in the summer. On the same floor, behind a door usually kept closed, was another part of the house and a fifth bedroom claimed by Auntie when she came for one of her visits. It was unbearably hot there in summer, glacial in winter. From a passageway outside of it, a narrow flight of steps led down to the kitchen and another flight up to the attic.

The dusty stillness of that shut-off part of the house was often broken by me, by the sound of my footsteps as I climbed the stairs to the attic, or by the dull buzz of flies trapped between screen and window in the bedroom, or by spasms of coughing and the muttering-to-herself fussing of Auntie on one of her visits, the one I feared might be without end.

She had chosen the room for herself before I was born and appeared to be gloomily satisfied with its discomforts: extremes of temperature, an iron bedstead with a thin mattress covered with stained ticking, a bare floor, and little else. Were some of the rugs she crocheted meant for the floors of her daughter's house? How did she dispose of the ones I had seen her make?

Behind the door that closed off that uncanny space, I pictured Auntie lying on her back in her bed, her eyes opened wide and unblinking, smoking cigarettes in the dark.

I spent rainy afternoons in the attic, treading warily on the rough planks that served as flooring, hopping over the holes in which I could glimpse shadowy crossbeams where the jagged edges met, and where I feared spiders might lurk. There were five or six small rooms whose walls ended halfway up, and I could look through them to their windows that hardly let in light, they were so covered with webs and dust. Boxes were stacked everywhere. There was a huge metal birdcage, a dressmaker's form, canes, a top hat, and a moth-eaten black dress coat. Books moldered in heaps, and trunks with lids too heavy for me to lift decayed in corners. Except for my footprints, dust covered everything.

On the top steps of a narrow flight of stairs, alongside a collection of faded postcards, were piles of *National Geographic* magazines. I looked through them again and again. As I turned the glossy pages, I was startled each time by the singularity of everything that lived, whether in seashells, houses, nests, temples, logs, or forests, and in the multitude of ways creatures shelter and sustain themselves.

One early afternoon—I had not yet learned to read—I was sitting on a step below the landing, an open book on my lap, inventing a story to fit the illustrations. It was raining. From the little table on which it sat in a dark corner at the foot of the staircase, I heard the telephone ringing. Uncle Elwood came from his study to answer it. "Mr. Fox?" I heard him ask in a surprised voice.

I flew up the stairs to my room, closed the door, and got under the bedclothes. Soon Uncle Elwood knocked on the door, saying the call had been from my father, Paul, who was in Newburgh, about to take a cab to Balmville. "Won't you open your door?" he asked me.

The word *father* was outlandish. It held an ominous note. I was transfixed by it. It was as though I had emerged from a dark wood into the sudden glare of headlights.

Uncle Elwood persuaded me at last to come out of my room. He looked back to make sure I was following him down the stairs. After the alarm set off in me when I heard "Mr. Fox," I felt flat and dull. In the living room I stared listlessly at a new *National Geographic* lying on the oak library table next to an issue of the *Newburgh News*, open to the page where the minister's weekly column appeared. On top of the big radio with a pinched face formed by various dials, on which we listened to *Amos and Andy*, there was a bronze grouping, a lion holding its paw, lifted an inch or so above the head of a mouse. I had gazed at it often, wondering if the lion was about to pat the mouse or kill it.

I had not longed for my father. I couldn't think how he had known where to find me.

I wandered into the hall, pausing before a large painting I had seen a thousand times, a landscape of the Hudson Valley. Dreaming my way into it, I walked among the hills, halted at a waterfall that hung from the lip of a cliff; in the glen below it there was an Indian village, feathery columns of smoke rising straight up from tepees. The painting was bathed in an autumnal light as yellow as butter, the river composed of tiny regular waves that resembled newly combed blue-gray hair, gleaming as though oiled.

I heard loud steps on the porch. My father suddenly burst through the doors carrying a big cardboard box. He didn't see me in the shadowed hall as he looked around for a place to set down the box.

In those first few seconds, I took in everything about him; his physical awkwardness, his height—he loomed like a flagpole in the dim light—his fair curly hair all tumbled about his head, and his attire, odd to me, consisting of a wool jacket different in fabric and pattern from his trousers. He caught sight of me, dropped the box on the floor, its unsealed flaps parting to reveal a number of books, and exclaimed, "There you are!" as if I'd been missing for such a long time that he'd almost given up searching for me. Then at last!—I'd turned up in this old house.

Not much he said during the afternoon he spent with me had the troubling force of those words, and their joking acknowledgment that much time had elapsed since my birth.

I felt compelled to smile, though I didn't know why.

I bent toward the books. I guessed by their bright colors that they were meant for me. Eventually Uncle Elwood read them all aloud: *Robin Hood, King Arthur and the Knights of the Round Table, Tom Sawyer, Water Babies, Aesop's Fables, A Child's Garden of Verses, The Jungle Books,* and *Treasure Island.*

At some happy moment, I lost all caution. When my father got down on all fours, I rode him like a pony.

It was twilight when he left. The rain had stopped. As he turned back on the bottom porch step to hold up his arm in a salute that seemed to take in the world, and before he stepped into the taxi he'd ordered to return for him, the sun emerged from a thick cloud cover and cast its reddish glow over his face as though he'd ordered that, too.

The next morning, I woke at first daylight and ran down the staircase to the living room in my nightclothes, knowing—against my wish to find him there—that I wouldn't.

From the earliest days of my time with him, Uncle Elwood read to me every evening. A few months after my fifth birthday he began to teach me to read. From being a listener—a standing I hadn't thought about until I had the means to change it—I became a reader.

The bookshelves in the living room held works of poetry, books about national and local history, and, as I recall, stories by Mark Twain and Rudyard Kipling, among others. I memorized "If," a poem by Kipling, and in historical sequence the names of the American presidents. I would recite aloud the poem and the presidential roll call, to elicit a look of pride on the minister's face.

I read a daily children's story in the Newburgh newspaper. It was accompanied by a drawing of a rabbit wearing a jacket and waistcoat, and the central character was an American version of Beatrix Potter's Peter Rabbit, but plumper, far more sanguine, and never exposed to the slightest serious danger. I read the funny papers on Sunday, the *Katzenjammer Kids, Moon Mullins, The Gumps, Maggie and Jiggs,* and *Harold Teen;* the last-named I disliked intensely, for reasons I don't recall.

I was free to read any book in the house, but what comes first to memory is my deciphering of the old postcards that lay in heaps at the top of the attic steps. Most had been mailed from foreign capitals before the Great War and showed vistas of Rome and Paris, Berlin and London. On the writing side, there were messages in the spidery but legible penmanship of those days. As I read them, I thought I could hear the ghostly utterances of the travelers, Uncle Elwood's long-departed kin.

Around the time I learned to read, a woman named Maria and her three-year-old daughter, Emilia, moved into the house. Uncle Elwood had hired her to cook and clean and to watch over his mother when he and I were out. She and her child settled into Auntie's bedroom.

When she came, Auntie used my bedroom, and I slept on a cot in the study. I hardly remember Maria. Uncle Elwood told me she had been born in a faraway country, Montenegro. But with no effort of memory Emilia's face appears instantly in my mind's eye, perhaps because among the few photographs I have from those years, there is one of the two of us.

In the photograph, she is sitting outdoors in my wicker rocking chair. Her legs, too short to reach the ground, stick straight out; her hands grip the rounded arms of the chair. Her black ringlets are clustered like Concord grapes around her little face. She is fretful. Her mouth forms an O. I am standing beside the chair. My left arm lies possessively along its curved back. I am looking down at her. My expression is troubled, angry.

Uncle Elwood takes the picture. He stands a few feet away from us. She has begun to cry in earnest, noisily. As usual, I tell myself. Her mother comes out of the house and picks her up, murmuring to her. Uncle Elwood joins me where I am standing beneath the branches of a crab-apple tree. He takes my reluctant hand. "Shall we go for a walk, Pauli?" he asks. I nod wordlessly.

Maria stayed with us for less than a year. Then, for reasons not explained to me or that I've forgotten, she placed Emilia in a Catholic ophanage and left Newburgh.

Uncle Elwood and I visited Emilia several times. A nun led us down a hall and into a barely furnished room smelling of floor wax, with starched white curtains at both windows. It was around noon. A distinct piercing smell that I recognized as beef broth floated in the air. One of the windows was open a crack, and a breeze kept the curtains waving like banners.

Emilia came into the room and sat down on a wooden bench, smiling uncertainly in our direction. She was dressed in a white blouse and a blue pinafore. Her curls were flattened by hair clips. She was probably four years old at the time. I don't know what we spoke about or if she spoke at all.

What I felt was the force of my longing to move into the orphanage that very hour. I wanted for myself the aroma of broth, the white starched curtains, the clothes Emilia wore, the nuns with their pale moon faces and black habits.

Emilia looked so calm, so *rescued*.

*   *   *

I grew aware that Uncle Elwood's public life consisted of more than preaching sermons. He wrote a weekly column for the *Newburgh News* called "Little-known Facts about Well-Known People." He told me that before he'd been called to the ministry, he'd been a journalist working for a newpaper in Portsmouth, Virginia.

I spelled out his name on the spines of several books set apart on the living room bookshelves. Among them were a history of the Blooming Grove church, a collection of his own sonnets, a biography of the twenty-fifth president of the United States, William McKinley, and a slim volume about the winter George Washington spent at his headquarters at Temple Hill, at that time a bare site not far south of Newburgh.

Years later, when a replica of the headquarters was erected, it was partly paid for with funds raised by the minister.

When Auntie visited, or during the months Maria worked for him, Uncle Elwood was free to explore the countryside and chase down clues to Hudson Valley history, many of them given to him by people in his congregation. One time he told me, an expression on his face that somehow combined horror and fastidiousness, how Indians had killed the infants of settlers by grabbing their feet and swinging them against tree trunks. He often quoted Washington's whispered question on his deathbed—so it had been reported—"Is it well with the child?" Uncle Elwood explained to me that the first president had meant the new country; the new country was the child. I repeated the words silently, not sure whether I meant the country or myself.

"We'll drive there like blazes!" he would declare, after he'd been told where there might be a foundation of a house built during the American Revolution or a tumbledown ruin that could have been built even earlier.

Once when we were walking in the woods somewhere, we stumbled upon an Indian burial ground, the mounds fallen in and covered with moss, and a light broke over his face. He treated the Hudson Valley and his ministry with the same ardor, as though both historical discovery and biblical allegory were equal manifestations of the divine.

We took trips.

We drove south to Nyack, a town on the western shore of the Hudson, to visit a cousin of Uncle Elwood's, who had recently had a house built for herself and a woman friend.

The river glinted in shards of light. Light-colored stones formed a promenade next to the house. The rooms were open, without doors; whiteness hung like a great curtain outside vast windows. The cousin's name was Blanche Frost.

She gave me a doll she told me she had bought in Paris.

"Where is Paris?" I asked the minister in a whisper, awed in the presence of the tall woman with such beautifully arranged white hair.

"Across the sea, in a country called France," he told me.

The doll's long yellow hair was held back from its face by a raspberry-colored ribbon, the same color as its startling dress, very short, revealing long light-pink cloth legs. I put it in my bookcase at home. For weeks, it was the last thing I looked at before I fell asleep.

We drove to Elmira, New York, to see Mark Twain's grave. It was a happy moment afterward, to sit in the sunlight on a nearby slope among the gravestones. The minister had on his high-crowned Panama hat, so it must have been August, the only month he wore it.

We went to Albany. In the governor's mansion, or the state-house, I forget which, the minister pointed to a deep scar in the banister of the broad staircase, made by a tomahawk hurled by a long-dead Indian.

We descended by elevator to the Howe caverns. The deep shaft down which we traveled looked like a giant's work; the earth split open just like the stones I had pounded on the long driveway.

One morning we were to go to West Point, where Uncle Elwood was to give an invocation at a military ceremony. We had to take the Storm King mountain road to get there. A snake coiled to strike would not have frightened me more than the snakelike curves of the road. At its highest point, where the rock face soared above and dropped to the river below, a sign warned of a zone of falling rocks. When we came to it, I drew up my legs and shut my eyes tight, expecting to be crushed by a boulder or flung out into space. When the road leveled out, I thought, This time we got away with it.

Uncle Elwood read me stories by Washington Irving, *Rip Van Winkle* and *The Legend of Sleepy Hollow*, out of whose pages a headless horseman pursued me into a dream. I told him I was haunted. Soon after, he took me to Sunnyside, Irving's estate near Tarrytown on the east side of the Hudson. Perhaps by showing me evidence of the writer's existence, he thought to exorcise the horseman.

In Balmville, just at the start of the dirt road that led home, there stood a very old Balm of Gilead tree encircled by an iron fence. Uncle Elwood told me that Washington was said to have taken shelter beneath its outstretched boughs during a sudden downpour. I could imagine the general standing there, looking as he did in a large portrait of him that hung in Uncle Elwood's study: cloaked, pink-cheeked, white-haired, with a marionette's stiffness of jaw. We often paused at the tree, the car motor idling, when we returned from our travels.

A mile or so away from the tree was the Delano home where we were once invited to tea. It was during the period when a family member, Franklin Delano Roosevelt, was governor of New York State. I might have forgotten the grandeur of the house and of the great winding staircase if I had not for the first time glimpsed the possibility of beauty in clothes, watching two little Delano girls hovering like butterflies about the table in white organdy dresses, slipping little cakes into their mouths.

We went to a neigboring town to attend a dinner given for a

bishop. He sat at the head of a long table. During a lull in the general conversation, I asked the bishop, "Do you like me?" and he replied, "Don't you think your question is a little premature?"

I was chagrined. Later, when Uncle Elwood smiled as he told people the story of my question and the bishop's response, I was confused by the currents of pride and shame running through me and felt a small pinch of estrangement from him.

Uncle Elwood wrote his sermons and newspaper columns on an Underwood typewriter on a table that stood in the middle of his study. It was a large, square, plain room with big windows. On fair days, when the light poured in, it seemed to float. Books lined one wall. Against another was an immensely tall desk that suggested a Chinese temple I had seen in an issue of the *National Geographic*. It had many tiny doors, which opened to dusty secret passages. In little drawers, mostly empty, there were piles of foreign coins, mementos of trips to Europe, and a piece of yellowed hardtack that Uncle Elwood told me dated from the Civil War. I would surprise myself with it, the last thing I examined before I got down from a high desk chair. I had to fight off an impulse to eat it.

On the wall beside the desk there hung a photograph of Edwin Markham, the poet, and he had written a few lines from his poem "The Man with the Hoe" in the open space beneath it. He had more beard than face. I invented a story: He was the missing one of the Smith Brothers whose cough drops came in a box illustrated with sketches of themselves, bearded and disembodied, that Uncle Elwood brought home for me when I had a sore throat or a cold.

Except for an occasional clatter of typewriter keys, there was a companionable silence between us. He asked me once, "What shall I preach about next Sunday, Pauli?"

"A waterfall," I replied at once. I had just been thinking about a recent picnic we had on the shore of a stream fed by a small cascade whose spray dampened our sandwiches and us.

I can still recall the startled pleasure I felt that Sunday in church when I realized his sermon was indeed about a waterfall. I grasped consciously for an instant what had been implicit in every aspect of daily life with Uncle Elwood—that everything counted and that a word spoken as meant contained a mysterious energy that could awaken thought and feeling in both speaker and listener.

An ancient parishioner, "old as the hills," Uncle Elwood observed, died in her sleep. He was named executor in her will. A few days after her funeral service in the church, we went to the Washingtonville boardinghouse where she had lived for many years. Her room had not been touched. The unmade bed, a half-pulled-out drawer in a small bureau, gave the place a disheveled look. Uncle Elwood walked across the dusty floor to a window, threw it open, and dusted his hands in a finicky way.

There was a hard-hearted aspect to his nature. Perhaps he had grown too accustomed to the dying, to death. We spent less than fifteen minutes in the room. He collected a few papers from a table and plucked, from a tangle of threads and spools in a sewing basket, a small ring with an amethyst stone that he gave me on the spot.

He spoke to the elderly landlady who was fluttering about in the hallway, asking her to pack Miss Hattie's things, keep whatever she liked, and give the rest to charity.

On our way home that day, he parked the car in front of a large house on the outskirts of Newburgh. Its roof formed steep hills, each one crowned with a chimney. Uncle Elwood sat in silence for a moment, his hands resting on the steering wheel.

Several years earlier, he told me, before he had brought me home to live with him, he had been on what he called a "thinking walk" in a field near Balmville. Suddenly he heard alarmed cries from a neighboring field. He turned to see that an untethered bull was about to heave itself at a young woman who, at that very second, hiked up her skirt and turned to run away from it. He diverted the animal by presenting himself s a target. The woman escaped and so did he. That was how he met Elizabeth, the person we were about to visit in the many-chimneyed house.

After the incident with the bull, they had become friends. A year or so later she fell ill and was now largely confined to her bed. Despite her loss of health, he proposed marriage to her. Regretfully, she refused him. All this was told to me in a tone in his voice I'd not heard before—elegiac, I tell myself now.

"Would you like to visit her?" he asked. I was curious and said yes. I couldn't conceive of him other than as a nurse to his mother, a savior for me, and the shepherd of what appeared—if I thought about it at all—as a world full of ungainly sheep stumbling along behind him, but never as someone's husband.

A maid opened the front door to us, and we followed her up a flight of stairs and into an enormous overheated bedroom crowded with furniture. A woman reclined in the bed against a pile of pillows almost as high as a hayrick. Her face was pale beneath her piled-up, silky-looking gray hair. Her thin listless hands lay on the coverlet. Her voice was pleasant and utterly assured.

Remembering its resonance, I now wonder if her illness, a thyroid imbalance, was itself the source of her self-confidence. After all, whatever its miseries, it had eliminated the necessity of making a choice, and the attendant anxiety that might have been aroused.

Her evident interest in me was puzzling. I grew conscious of my breathing and aware at the same time that I felt alone, cut off from Uncle Elwood. I moved to his side. For a while I was relieved that Elizabeth had turned his proposal down.

* * *

Laughter erupted from Uncle Elwood like a Roman candle, and at its peak he might exclaim, in a choked voice, "Killing!"

I learned I could evoke his laughter by imitating people, especially old Mr. Howell. There were other ways I contrived to set him off, some more successful than others.

One day he brought home a dog, a chow with bushy rust-colored fur and a tongue as black as licorice. He called him Ching. The dog was amiable, if reserved, with me.

On an early evening, Uncle Elwood drove to Newburgh to do an errand and took me along. Ching sat on the backseat, and I joined him there after Uncle Elwood had parked and left the car with his customary quickness of movement.

The dog was wagging his tail in a leisurely fashion. Uncle Elwood's gray suede gloves were lying where he had tossed them on the seat. One thing led to another. I pulled a glove down over Ching's tail and hid on the car floor, murmuring to Ching so he would keep up his tail wagging, hugging myself in anticipatory glee as I visualized Uncle Elwood's face when he caught sight of a hand waving at him through the rear window.

I heard his rapid returning steps on the sidewalk. He paused a few feet from the car. It was absolutely still outside. I nearly shrieked. Then the door opened. "Pauli!" he exclaimed in apparent astonishment, his eyes crinkling with laughter.

In later years, I realized that Ching and I hadn't fooled him for an instant, that what his laughter had expressed was appreciation of my cunning as he stood near the car, his attention momentarily caught by the flicker of a slowly waving gray hand.

On a September morning a few months after my fifth birthday, the minister drove me to the public school a mile or so away. After a few weeks, I was allowed to walk home with the four or five children who lived along the road.

Miss Hamilton taught first grade. She was plump and friendly. Her hair was bound about her head like a black silk scarf. Her dark eyes were large and slightly protuberant.

Three classmates stand out in my memory from those days: Lester, a tall farmer's son who wore the same faded overalls every day—I realized this when I noticed the same stains in the same places—and who had grayish skin and a wedge-shaped head he held stiffly as he slouched and shambled around the classroom; Lucy, who became a friend; and Freddie Harrison, in whose presence I often lost my breath and was unable to speak. How did Uncle Elwood know about the joyful consternation I felt in those moments when Freddie and I passed by each other in the classroom or stood silently together in the school playground?

One warm afternoon, Lucy came to visit me. We drew what we conjectured to be male genitals on the blank backs of paper dolls, our heated faces close together as we crouched under a yellow-leafed maple tree near the stone wall. I don't know what we were hiding from unless it was our own prescience of sexual love. In any event, we weren't far off the mark.

I had a curious view of the world and its inhabitants. I imagined people were lodged inside the earth like fruit pits, and I was perplexed by the visible sky. Miss Hamilton substituted an even stranger view, that we all lived upon the earth's surface. How was it we didn't fall and tumble forever through space?

I walked home with the other children on the dirt road. It curved steeply at its beginning, and on the rise we passed a fieldstone house in a huddled mass of trees that hid it from sunlight. It looked emptier of life than the little graveyard behind it, where two or three tombstones had fallen over onto the ground. It all had a brooding character that stirred and frightened me. Its lightless windows looked like the eyes of a blind dog.

Gradually the other children glided away, down paths or rutted roadways, their faces assuming a certain blankness of expression they would wear indoors for the first minutes after they reached home, as my face did, until there was only one left, Gordon, a tall boy with a cap of black curls, who lived a half mile beyond my driveway and with whom I walked in an easy silence.

Car headlights shone on ranks of stunted pine trees and clumps of small weathered gray houses, silent, silvered for an instant as we drove past them. Who was driving, Uncle Elwood or my father, I can't recall. We were on our way to Provincetown at the tip of Cape Cod, where my parents were living in a house on Commercial Street. Soon after my stay of a few days, when they were away, it burned to the ground—the fourth fire started by the retarded son of a Portuguese fisherman.

The house, a saltbox, was set back from the street a few hundred feet on the hummocky undernourished ground characteristic of land near salt water. I have a snapshot of myself standing in front of a straggly rosebush growing on a rickety trellis in the yard, its stems like insect feelers. There is another photograph of Uncle Elwood and me by the bay. He kneels to hold me around the waist, although there is no surf; the water is as flat as an ironing board. I suppose my father took the picture with the minister's camera.

A German shepherd my parents owned attacked a cat that was drifting along the narrow cracked sidewalk in front of the house. My heart thudded; my vision narrowed to the two animals, one helpless, the other made monstrous with rage. I grabbed the cat. In its terror, it scratched my hand.

There was no one in the house that day to whom I could report the scratch. I washed my hand at the kitchen sink, standing on a chair to turn on the faucet. The wound bled intermittently for a while. When my parents returned from wherever they had been, I didn't bring it to their attention.

I discovered a steamer trunk in a little room next to the kitchen. It was on end and partly open, like a giant book waiting to be read. Deep drawers lined one side. Suits and dresses hung in the other. They looked as though they'd been pitched across the room, arrested in their flight by small hangers attached to a metal bar, to which they clung, half on, half off.

I had never seen so many women's clothes before. I touched them, felt them, pressed against them, breathing in their close bodily smell until I grew dizzy. I pulled open a drawer and discovered a pile of cosmetics.

I hardly knew what they were for, but memories stirred of Uncle Elwood's mother, asking that her face be powdered when she was about to be taken for an outing in the car and a large powder puff in his hand as he bent toward her face, or the lips of some of his parishioners, too red to be true.

My mother was suddenly in the room, as though deposited there by a violent wind. I gasped with embarrassment and fear. She began to speak; I saw her lips move. I bent toward her, feeling the fiery skin of my face.

"What are you doing?" She was asking me over and over again. I heard her repeat "doing . . . doing" in the same measured voice, as she stared at my forehead covered with her powder, at my mouth, enlarged and thickened with lip rouge I had discovered in a tiny circular box.

I began to cry silently. Her face loomed in front of mine like a dark moon. She began to whisper with a kind of ferocity, "Don't cry! Don't you dare! Don't! Don't cry!"

I covered my face with my hands. She pushed in the trunk drawers and straightened the clothes. I sensed that if she could have hidden the act, she would have killed me.

I stood there, waiting for permission to stay or to leave. She left the room as though I weren't there.

There was a party that evening. The noise of it came up the narrow stairs to the alcove where I lay on a cot, listening. It was like the sound of the ocean roaring in a seashell.

Grandfather Fox appeared at the Balmville house one afternoon. I sat on his bony lap and asked him why he sometimes whistled as he spoke. "False teeth," he replied.

I couldn't recall seeing him before. He seemed pleasant if close-mouthed. I wondered if it was because he didn't know me despite the fact that there I was, sitting on his lap. Perhaps I was being premature, as I had been with the bishop.

Then he said to Uncle Elwood, with no reproach in his voice, "You are ruining my son," and I understood that until that moment he had been holding back those words as if they were hard little pebbles, rolling around in his mouth. I didn't understand what they meant.

When I was a few years older, my father told me his father had attended a German university, where he had taken a degree in philosophy. Most of the other students had saber scars on their faces from the duels they had fought.

My grandmother Fox, Mary Letitia Finch, had been one of five sisters, my father said. When admirers came to court them, their father would stomp into the living room, lift out a sword hanging in its scabbard over the fireplace mantel, and brandish it at them.

One daughter, Sara Finch, had packed a footlocker at the age of fifty and moved to the Bowery in New York City, where she made the acquaintance of a sailor at a tavern. She lived with him a year until he found a desirable berth on a ship bound for South America. She then returned to her father's house and proceeded to write love letters, signing the sailor's name to them and mailing them to herself. She greeted their arrival with cries of joy if her father was nearby.

My father recalled that another Finch sister had eloped with a Hungarian Jew. They had a child and named him Douglas, a family name. He grew up and became an actor, Douglas Fairbanks. He was my father's first cousin.

When Grandfather Fox returned from Germany to the United States, he had been able to find work only as a traveling salesman, a drummer, selling medical supplies, going from town to town lugging a huge black sample case.

My grandmother's tyrannical father had felt that his daughter had married beneath her when her husband became a traveling salesman, although when he was a philosopher he didn't consider that she had.

One morning when my grandfather left the family home for a week of peddling in Pennsylvania, my father, then a small boy, hid behind a tree and threw an apple core at him, shouting, "Red! Red!" at his redheaded father. He desperately didn't want him to go away on still another trip for what must have seemed to him a year.

* * *

Shortly after my grandfather's visit, the minister drove me to Yonkers, to Warburton Avenue, where my Aunt Jessie Fox and my grandparents lived in a tall, narrow wooden house. I looked forward to the visit with curiosity and apprehension.

My aunt had thin freckled hands and a slight hump below her right shoulder, which gave her an air of impending wickedness. It was a result, Daddy said, of an early bout with tuberculosis. She smoked continually. Often, as she spoke, she twisted and twirled her hands about. She was ten years older than her brother, my father, and, like him, had a beautiful voice, but she talked constantly, and it became beautifully monotonous.

She led me through the many rooms of the house. They were either empty or crowded with furniture. In the long living room, on the wall behind a small sofa, hung a gold-framed mirror. It diminished the size of all that it reflected, and showed a scene as tiny and perfect and lifeless as a village inside a spun-sugar Easter egg I had once seen somewhere. When I looked away from it to the real room I was in, I realized how shabby and forlorn the furnishings were.

Someone very old was sitting in a large chair in front of a table at the end of the room. She was wrapped in many scarves and a blanket but had worked one of her arms loose so she could do the crossword puzzle in a newspaper that lay on her lap. From time to time, she raised her head and stared into the distance through thick-glassed spectacles.

"Here's little Paula, Mother," Aunt Jessie said.

The old woman made a comment. I've forgotten the words, but I recall her voice, soft and cold and small, a sound that might have issued from something that lived on the bottom of the sea.

Later that day, I sat at my aunt's dressing table letting a necklace of bright glass beads flow from hand to hand. She told me the necklace had come from Venice, a city in Italy that floated upon water.

She spoke about my father's restlessness when he'd been a boy. She had waked many mornings just before dawn to discover her little brother, unable to sleep through the night, curled up on the floor beneath her bed. On other nights, he slept under his parents' bed. "Even in winter when it's so cold?" I asked her, startled by the image of him in a nest of dust and cobwebs. "Even in winter," she replied.

I noted that day how she spoke of men as "the little fellows," but when she mentioned my father it was always by his name, Paul. "The little fellows came to repair our plumbing but they didn't do so well," she remarked when I told her that the faucet in the bathroom was leaking.

At one point, she recalled an incident that involved her brother and began to smile. When my father was ten or so, he was standing beside her at a window that looked out on the skimpy lawn at the front of the house. It was a summer evening, and she was waiting for a suitor to call. As the young man came into view, walking up the cement path to the porch,

Paul, who had not seen him before, made a derisive remark about him.

My aunt had laughed. She was laughing as she told me about it, and had laughed as she had gone to the front door, opened it, and given the young man his "walking papers." She could no longer remember his name.

My grandmother lived to be 101, kept alive, my father told me some years later, by his sister's desperate measures. Jessie was like a living bellows, breathing air, day after day, into the ancient woman's exhausted lungs. When her mother died, Jessie began to slide into a state of senile dementia and was taken off to a local nursing home where, unless restrained, she bit her nurses when they attended her. She was carried out of life one day in a fit of deranged anger. My grandfather had died in his eighties, long before his wife and daughter, from what, I don't know; but I attributed to him as his last conscious emotion—unjustly, perhaps—relief at leaving behind him his deplorable family.

I drove past the house decades later. Warburton Avenue led to an old scenic drive along the east bank of the Hudson River. The front door was boarded up. It looked abandoned. I wondered who would be so desperate for housing that they would buy it.

A year passed between the long drive to Provincetown and several visits I made to apartments where my parents stayed in New York City, one visit to a rented cabin in the

Adirondack Mountains, and a few hours in a restaurant on the Coney Island boardwalk, midday in the spring.

A scene occurred there that displayed the pleasure my mother, Elsie, took in her own mockery. I was sitting at a table with her and my father and several of their acquaintances. A small band was playing popular songs of the day. She turned to me suddenly. Would I go over to the bandstand and request a song called "Blasé?"

I felt excitement at the thought of carrying out her wish, but I was abashed by her smile of amusement and the secret it implied.

I made my way among the tables to the bandleader, who was in the middle of a number. I stood beside the bandstand where the musicians sat in scissorlike wooden chairs, blowing and fiddling on their instruments. At last I caught the eye of the bandleader. My voice to him must have been nearly inaudible. What I said was, " 'Blasé' for *her*," and pointed to the table where my mother was sitting. His sour expression gave way to a startled smile. He waved in her direction and bowed slightly. Everyone was laughing: my parents and their friends, people at tables close enough to the platform to have heard my request, and now the conductor himself. My face blazed. I knew, without understanding what it was, that their laughter was about something ridiculous I had done.

* * *

My parents were staying temporarily—their arrangements, as far as I could work out, were permanently temporary—in a small borrowed apartment in New York City. The minister arranged with my father to leave me there for a few hours and then return to take me home.

A large dog lay on the floor, its eyes watchful. I recognized it as the same animal that had attacked the cat in Provincetown a year or so earlier. It got up to sniff my shoes. My father filled in the silence with his voice. I wasn't listening to him. Where was my mother?

Suddenly she appeared in the doorway that led to a second room. I saw an unmade bed behind her. She pressed one hand against the doorframe. The other was holding a drink. My father's tone changed; his voice was barely above a whisper. "Puppy . . . puppy . . . puppy," he called her softly, as though he feared, but hoped, to wake her. She stared at me, her eyes like embers.

All at once she flung the glass and its contents in my direction. Water and pieces of ice slid down my arms and over my dress. The dog crouched at my feet. My father was in the doorway, holding my mother tight in his arms. Then he took me away from the apartment.

At some hour he must have returned with me. Perhaps we waited for the minister outside the front door.

For years I assumed responsibility for all that happened in my life, even for events over which I had not the slightest control. It was not out of generosity of mind or spirit that I did so. It was a hopeless wish that I would discover why my birth and my existence were so calamitous for my mother.

A few months later Uncle Elwood took me to the city again to visit my parents. This time they were staying in a hotel owned by a family they were acquainted with, whose wealth included vast land tracts on the west side of the Hudson River, just north of the Palisades, as my father explained to me. I was to stay overnight, and for that purpose the rich family provided a room for me across the corridor from Paul and Elsie.

The idea of spending so much time with them filled me with alarm. But the visit began cheerfully, though a malaise gripped me as soon as I saw them together in the hotel room. I mistook the feeling for excitement.

Humorously, my parents played with the idea that I should marry the son of the hotel owners, a boy only a year or so older than I was, I guessed. They would arrange the marriage first thing in the morning, they promised, both smiling broadly. I strained to match their mood. It would be like the marriages of children in India. I had seen such children in an issue of the *National Geographic*. They looked so little. They wore bands of jewels across their brows and large brilliantly colored flowers behind their ears.

Evening approached. The dark, like ink, filled up the air-shaft of their room on the fourteenth floor. My father asked me what I would like for supper; he would order it from room service. My experience was only with the minister's cooking. "Lamb chop and peas," I said, partially aware that this was a special occasion: hotel rooms, Paul and Elsie, so tall, so slender, both, a marriage planned for the future so I would be able to live in this room for years, the excitement of great things about to happen. We hardly ever had lamb chops at Uncle Elwood's house, though we often had little canned peas. When the tray was delivered by a waiter, I looked at it and saw I had forgotten something.

"There's no milk," I observed.

At once, my father carried the tray to the window, opened it, and dropped the tray into the airshaft.

Moments later, as I stood there stunned by what my father had done—nothing Elsie did ever surprised me—I heard the tray crash. Through tight lips, my father said mildly, "Okay, pal. Since it wasn't to your pleasure . . . ." My mother, behind the half-closed door of the bathroom, where she had gone at the very moment he walked to the window, exclaimed "Paul!" in a muffled voice, as though she spoke through a towel.

Again, as in the episode of the trunk in Provincetown, I was profoundly embarrassed, as though I were implicated in my father's act. But nearly as painful was the gnawing hunger I suddenly felt for that lamb chop lying fourteen stories below.

As the two of them were leaving for the evening, for whatever entertainment they anticipated, there was a loud knocking at the door. My father opened it to a laughing young man, possessed by what was to me an inexplicable merriment. "Foxes!" he cried, clapping his hands, fluttering and capering, calling out praises to my mother. "Your costume, darling!" My father murmured, "Dick is to keep an eye on you," and at that the young man spotted me and held out his hand, which I took. "Come along, Paula," he called, even though I was standing next to him.

I followed him across the corridor to another room. He threw himself down on one of the twin beds, still smiling. "Well, dear little one. What shall we play?" he said, and promptly closed his eyes and fell asleep. Even if it had not been his purpose, he had rescued me from two incomprehensible people. I looked over at his pretty sleeping face in the other bed, and I was overcome with an emotion I had no word for—a kind of love for that stranger.

I put myself to sleep with pictures of everything I could envisage in the Balmville house, the way I felt its walls around me, and Uncle Elwood, coming and going; the animated spirit of it all.

It seems unlikely that I would have been allowed to go unaccompanied on a train to New York City, yet in the winter of 1928, you could place a child safely in the care of a conductor or a porter. In any event, several months after the Visit of the Dropped Tray, as I named it in my thoughts, I went to the city on the train and was met at Grand Central Station, not by my father but by a married couple, actors, who took me to their tiny apartment, which they shared with two enormous dogs—Great Danes, they told me. A large window in the living room looked out on Central Park.

They both had roles in the play *Animal Crackers*, and except on matinee days they were always at home during the day. They expected my father to "turn up" at any moment, as they smilingly told me. I spent two nights with the actors, going to sleep in their bedroom, carried into the living room and deposited on a sofa when they were ready to retire.

During the day the dogs kept watch over the two rooms, pacing restlessly the length of the living room or sleeping sluggishly in great canine heaps.

My father came to get me on a matinee day as the actors were on their way out the door. "Thanks, dear pals," he said to them. He told me he had lifted a few too many glasses two evenings earlier and had not been able to meet me at the station. "I was—ahem, ahem—indisposed," he said, with comical exaggeration, and I, without comprehending what he meant, smiled up at him. Now we were going to take a bus to Schroon Lake, New York, in the Adirondack Mountains, where he and my "sainted mother" had rented a cabin. I puzzled over his words about Elsie for a while, then gave it up as another mystery.

He looked tired, as though the glasses he had lifted had weighed too much for him. His water-color eyes were bloodshot; his voice, usually so deep, so melodic, as though he were always on the point of breaking into song, had a cranky, querulous note; and his words, usually so finely cut, were blurred.

He slept on the bus, falling against me as it lurched. I had not seen him since he had dropped the supper tray out the window, and I felt wary and nervous. As he slept, I investigated his face, his hands, one of which held an unlit cigarette, his trembling eyelids.

After hours of traveling, we arrived in the hamlet of Schroon Lake. My mother and a friend, a slender, spidery, dark-haired man, were waiting in front of a general store, a dusty, cheese-smelling, dark space in front of which stood a single gas pump. Nearby was a beat-up little car that apparently belonged to my parents. As I stepped from the bus, the spidery man's eyes widened with amusement. "Oh, she's a one!" he exclaimed to Elsie.

We drove several miles and turned off the paved road to a rutted lane. Soon a small cabin appeared. Behind it was Schroon Lake. A pale strip of shoreline was still visible, but it vanished as night spread over the water. The cabin was meagerly furnished; the smell of old fires emanated from a stove that stood at one end of the living room.

Recalling the evening in the hotel, I said nothing about meals, although I was hungry. My father fixed me supper with particular effort, noticeable effort, as if he too remembered that evening and was determined to erase it from both our memories. He laughed and talked ceaselessly. Now that I think of it, his movements and gestures might have been a dance of contrition.

The next evening we drove to the hamlet of Schroon Lake, parking the car on a country road across the street from a wooden building that served various community purposes that included movie showings. In the one that we saw Warner Baxter played the lead. When the film was over, I walked beside Elsie into the small anteroom that served as a lobby.

I startled myself by asking her how babies were made. The spidery man on her other side burst into laughter. After a moment, she replied, in an impersonal voice, "Sexual intercourse." At that moment, we reached the car. She drove, with my father in the passenger seat and the spidery man and me in the rear. She spoke animatedly about other matters. No one mentioned the movie or my question and her answer.

Suddenly, as it seemed to me then, my childhood years with Uncle Elwood and his mother ended. Plans of which I had been ignorant came to fruition. My father, who was living in California, sent for me. I found myself on a train with Aunt Jessie bound for Los Angeles.

Outside of Albuquerque, New Mexico, a dozen or so cowboys galloped alongside the train, slapping the flanks of their horses with their broad-brimmed hats as they yipped. The train gathered speed and the cowboys fell away, one by one, their cries fading gradually as though blotted up by the vast sky.

One night the train slowed as it passed through a village. Through the window, I saw a tree-lined lane lit by rays of a street-lamp. I longed to be walking along it past the shadowed houses, on my way home in the silent dark.

I spent a year or so in California. When I came back, it was winter in the East. There was snow on the ground when I returned to Balmville and Uncle Elwood.

It was to be for only a few more months. I held on to the transient safety. I knew it to be a lifeline that might slip out of my hands at any moment.

One gray winter afternoon before I left for good, my friend Lucy and I went to skate on a small frozen pond not far from the Balmville tree.

Out of cold blue shadows, from beneath tall leaning ice-stiffened reeds, a boy emerged with a hockey stick held diagonally before him. Another boy appeared behind the first, then another. They looked like medieval warriors. As Lucy and I watched from the pond's edge, a black puck flew out from under their skates like a crow, and slid along the thick pearly ice.

Hollywood

Sober or drunk, my father spoke dismissively about the places he had lived in over the years. After downing a few drinks, he would fall in love with his own voice, theatrically honeyed, filled with significant whispers and pauses. He was in thrall to his voice; his thoughts stumbled behind.

From fragments of sentences that fell from his lips, I understood him to be claiming that he'd been on his way to his true and noble destination when he was sidetracked by women. He himself, he asserted, would have been contented with an unadorned life, a roof over his head to shelter him from weather, a cot to sleep on, a stove to keep him warm when cold winds blew, and upon which he could prepare spartan meals.

All men aspire toward the mountain peaks, but women drive them down into valleys of domesticity where they are ambushed by family life and other degrading and petty tyrannies.

As we drew near to his rented house in the car he had met

us with at the Los Angeles railroad station, he gestured toward it, saying disdainfully that it was furnished with "yard upon yard of Spanish junk." The road we were on ended a half a mile farther among bare hills. At their summit rose a gigantic sign: HOLLYWOODLAND.

When I recall the few days I spent at the house, I'm always outdoors and it is nighttime. The dark is thinned by stepping stones of amber light cast on the sidewalk by streetlamps. The house is large, its windows partially hidden by elaborate ironwork grilles. An outside staircase reaches the top floor. Big shadowed houses stand back from the street, separated by extensive gardens and trees unfamiliar to me.

Aunt Jessie, her task to deliver me to California completed, departed after a week or so for the East and her mother, whom she'd left in a housekeeper's care. On the evening of the day she boarded a train bound for New York, Daddy and my mother went out to a party, leaving me on my own.

In the long dusk, I wandered through doorless, cavelike rooms with beamed ceilings and rough white plaster walls, turning on lights where I could reach a switch. A chill rose from the red tiles of the floor. Tables and chairs were made of some dark wood. A plump pink sofa squatted in the center of one of the larger rooms. The sudden barking of a dog startled me, each bark like a gunshot.

I came to the front door, opened it, and stepped outside. It swung shut behind me. I tried the metal handle. Even as I moved it back and forth, I knew I was locked out.

The dark tightened around me, and for a moment I couldn't draw breath. It was as if the night were a black sack into which I'd been dropped. I listened. A faint breeze rustled the leaves of the trees; a car suddenly speeded up with a grinding of gears on an unseen street. There was the steady splash of a waterfall at the back of the house. I tiptoed toward it across the grass.

It fell into a shallow pool like a serpent sliding from a tree branch, the water shimmering in the lights from the house. In the pool swam a few torpid goldfish. I had spent hours beside that pool, and one morning I had fallen into it.

A man appeared suddenly a few feet away. His head was cocked at an angle as though he too were listening. When he saw me, he said—and his voice surprised me in a world only seconds ago empty of human life—"I've made the same mistake before. I think I've left on my lawn sprinkler. Then I find out it's the sound of your little waterfall." He waved toward it.

"I'm locked out," I told him.

He nodded in agreement. He seemed to know that no one was home. He said, "We'll go to my house. Are you hungry?" I said yes, though I wasn't. He held out his hand and I took it. We walked a short distance to his house.

In the kitchen, his wife sliced a banana into a bowl. I ate it at the kitchen table, observed by their grave, friendly faces. When I'd finished the banana, I was so sleepy I could hardly hold my head up. The wife led me up a staircase to a spare bedroom, unused since their son had grown up and moved to another state to live and work. I crawled beneath the sheet in my underwear, and she drew up a quilt over me. I was nearly asleep when she whispered she had made the quilt herself.

It was warm, bright with color. My last thought was of Joseph's coat, which I'd heard about in Sunday school in Uncle Elwood's church.

Early the next morning, I walked back to my parents' house and climbed up the outside steps to a door. It was unlocked. I opened it, at the same time calling, "Daddy!"

From one of two beds, a blanket rose into the air like a large animal getting to its four feet. Suddenly my father was holding me like a rag doll and running down the back stairs. His pajama top was unbuttoned. I glimpsed patches of pale skin as we entered the kitchen where a black maid was ironing. He seemed unaware of her presence as he whirled about looking for a chair. What he'd wanted was to get me out of the bedroom.

I knew it wasn't my mother in the other bed. I'd seen yellow hair on the pillow.

He lighted on a chair, put me across his knees, and began to spank me.

"Mr. Fox! That isn't right! It isn't fair!" the black maid protested.

My father looked up at her as if surprised by her presence. I was astonished that she had defended me and lifted my head from his knee to stare at her. Years later, when I thought about her—and I thought about her often—about how much she had had to overcome in the way of an enforced and habitual discretion, how a sense of justice in her had outweighed the risk—I realized how brave she had been.

A decade after the incident, my father told me, in what he deemed to be a comical voice, that that night he had pretended to be a childless bachelor and had "brought home a girl from the party." Then I had burst into the bedroom at a heathen hour of the morning, shouting "Daddy!"

I never discovered where my mother had spent the night. Nor did my father ask me where I had been before I opened the door to the bedroom.

A few days later, my father drove me to Redlands, a small town thirty-five or forty miles from Hollywood. He left me there in the care of an old woman, Mrs. Cummings. She kept house for Sophie, her enormous daughter, who ran a summer camp for girls in the Big Bear Mountains.

One morning before I went off to school, I had just sat down on the edge of my bed to put on my shoes when the house shuddered, tipped forward and backward, and pitched me to the floor. At that instant, Mrs. Cummings called out, her voice sounding like a cat's cry of distress. I crawled to the front door. It had been wrenched from its hinges and lay upon the narrow wooden porch. In the middle of the street, in front of the house, smoking with clouds of dust, a deep crevice had opened. No one was out of doors. I stood up and ran to the kitchen, where I found Mrs. Cummings crouching beneath the kitchen table, looking straight ahead with a crazed glare. "Get under here," she muttered.

We sat beneath the table, our knees touching, the closest we'd been in all the months preceding the earthquake. There was another great shake of the house; for a few seconds the walls undulated like cloth.

Gradually, as the silence deepened around us, her expression grew focused. It conveyed that there was no language to describe what had just occurred. For moments, the world's heart had stopped.

After minutes—it could have been hours—she crept out from under the table, revealing her pink bloomers to me as the skirt of her dress tangled with her legs. Human cries began to reach us from the street. I went again to the porch. Families, solitary people, dogs, stood in front of their houses staring down at the great wound in the street from which now issued several muddy, slow-moving streams of water.

I wondered if the chameleon Mrs. Cummings had given me a week earlier had survived. The last time I had seen it, a few days before, it was pausing in front of a mousehole in the kitchen baseboard, staring at it with its right eye. When I looked back a minute later, it had vanished.

Since then, I had thought about it constantly, its sudden stillnesses, its skittering about, its tiny clawed feet on my skin, the way it turned the color of what it was placed upon. "I hope it finds something to eat," I said to Mrs. Cummings. "It's fine," she replied. "Living in the cellar . . . eating flies." I didn't believe her but didn't say so.

A terror of leprosy leapt into my soul. I looked under my bed every night in case there was a leper sleeping there. Leprosy was the most awful thing in the world. Tidal waves ran a close second.

I sat on a high stool in front of the kitchen sink, staring down at an egg I had broken to find out how its inside got inside. The orange yolk bled into the drain; a gelatinous white mass followed the yoke sluggishly. Mrs. Cummings entered the kitchen and began to reproach me for wasting an egg. I wasn't listening. I was recalling the way I had cracked open stones on the long driveway that led up to the minister's house on the hill. I grew weak with longing to be in the downstairs hall where we had all gathered during storms, to see old Mrs. Corning; even Auntie; most of all, Uncle Elwood.

Sophie was director of a camp in the mountains called Tamarack Lodge. One weekend morning in early spring—though I couldn't tell the months apart in that country without seasons—Sophie and Jay, the man who did the maintenance work in the camp, drove to the lodge and took me along. Jay was heavy-set and looked unshaven by mid-morning. When I saw him, he was always wearing a plaid shirt drawn tightly over his big belly.

The campgrounds were silent. The shuttered main house, the swimming pool emptied of water, its bottom covered with evergreen needles, a line of boarded-up cabins, and the boulder- and rockstrewn thickly treed hills that rose all around had a thrilling look of desolation. Jay and Sophie talked in low voices as they walked about, pausing in front of various buildings, their faces serious.

A decade later when I returned to California from the East, one of the first things I did was to take a bus to the village near the campgrounds. It was December and chilly, and patches of old hardened snow were on the ground. I didn't know if the camp would still be there. I walked from the village on a narrow road until I came upon a gravel driveway that led beneath an arch with the camp's name on it in rustic letters. I wandered around for a while. A stream, full this time of year, formed a natural barrier at one side of the camp. It tumbled and sang in the silence. A memory slid into my mind.

One summer day when I was six, I was riding in the open back of a camp truck and, egged on by the older girls, I hit a child smaller than I was. She was odd-looking. Her lips were nearly invisible and her teeth protruded. I didn't have a reason—there never is one—except the illusion that I would thus gain favor with the others. She cried out; her hand flew to her cheek. At that very moment, Sophie, sitting in the truck's passenger seat, glanced back at us through the dust-streaked window.

When we reached the general store where we would buy fruit and sandwiches for our picnic, Sophie led me to the bathroom at the back, sat down on a toilet seat, and placed me across her lap, all this without a word. She spanked me, and I welcomed the punishment as much as I could. I had committed a bully's crime.

Years later, I told my father that I had returned to the camp when I was sixteen. He said, "Ah, well . . . people who've been parceled out and knocked around are always returning to the past, retracing their steps." He spoke distantly, in a detached voice.

It was during that same exchange that he told me what my mother had said—after I'd spent a week or so in Hollywood in the house with the waterfall—which had resulted in his leaving me in old Mrs. Cummings's care.

"She gave me an ultimatum," he began. "She said, 'Either *she* goes or I go.' " He shook his head ruefully. "I had no choice," he said, in a faintly self-pitying tone of voice.

"I had only a few days to find someone to take care of you." Then he repeated his words: "I had no choice."

Along with the other younger children in the camp, I dug for gold in the bank that rose from the stream. Sophie explained that it was "fool's gold," a glittering pyrite, that we were unearthing. The others wandered off. I went on digging as though my life depended upon it, as though I were tunneling out of a prison.

One free-time afternoon, I explored the other side of the stream, crossing it where flattened stones formed a kind of watery bridge. Although I was watchful, on the lookout for mountain lions, whose roars at night I had heard, and my skin prickled at the swoosh of wings as a bird flew from one tree to another and at the scrabbling sound of a chipmunk running up a tree trunk, I persisted.

After a while, I came to a dip in the hills and, in it, a village. I walked down the middle of the only street. Nothing stirred, not even a leaf on a straggly tree next to the saloon with its swinging half-doors. There was something odd about this place. I looked up. Windows on upper floors framed blue squares of sky. Behind the church, the boardinghouses, the store, a sheriff's office, were huge braces supporting what were only fronts.

It was so unexpected to come across it, so mysterious. When I told Sophie about it, she said it was a movie set no longer in use. Like fool's gold, I told myself years after, so false in its promise, so real in itself.

Every weekday I walked several long blocks to the public school I attended in the flat, dusty little town. On my way there, I passed a large weedy lot. One morning, policemen were all over it, staring at the ground. The headless body of a child I'd known by sight had been discovered the afternoon before. Her head had been found stuffed into her book bag.

I learned that if I were to see my parents, I had to live away from them. The four or five times I visited them during that year I spent in Redlands, Mrs. Cummings would put me on a train to Los Angeles, placing me in the charge of a porter. Once, a friend of my father's, Vin Lawrence, met the train. He drove directly from the station to an all-night miniature golf course. It was brightly lit up, like a small-town circus. Vin loved golf, which he called "the green mistress."

He talked to me as if I were grown up, in a voice that sounded like soft barking. Now and then he whistled or made popping sounds with his mouth and clapped his small hands together—especially when his stroke had been good—resting the golf club he was using against one leg. He explained that my father had been unable to meet me because he had "lifted a few too many glasses," an explanation I had heard before that wasn't one.

He played the little course with utmost seriousness as I walked or waited beside him. He kept up a running commentary. A story about my mother held my attention. He called her "Spain."

He and my father had searched for and found an elegant black gown for her to wear to a movie opening at Grauman's

Chinese. They didn't know she had spent the day stuffing herself with olive oil and garlic on dark bread, food for which she had been suddenly possessed by intense longing. She arrived at the theater in time, wearing the velvet gown but stinking to high heaven. It was the first story I'd heard about her. Until then I had had only my own stories.

Another time, no one met the train. It was early evening. I sat for a while on a station bench, a small suitcase next to me. I worked out the words on a sign over a booth a few yards away. TRAVELER'S AID, it read.

I was a traveler and I needed aid. I went over. I don't recall any conversation, but I do remember the outcome. The woman behind the booth gave me taxi fare, and she smiled as she put the bills in both my hands.

My parents moved to Malibu Beach, where they rented a house built to look like the midsection of a small ship. A deck jutted out over the sand. At the top there was a large square room, like a captain's bridge, my father said, from which I could see the vast ocean.

I spent several weekends at the Malibu house. At a fated hour all the mornings I was there, my father gripped my resistant hands and lifted me over the foaming waves of the surf toward the dreadful green waters of the Pacific, into which he dropped me.

I sank at once, then rose, running in the water, keeping afloat in a way that every second left me in doubt about whether I would live to the next. I heard myself gasping and sputtering; it frightened me further. I knew there were miles of water-filled space below me. The only thing keeping me above it was the frenzied movement of my feet. "I'm drowning!" I'd cry. "No you aren't!" my father called out in a hard, jocular voice from a few yards away. And I wasn't.

Malibu was a beach movie palace. Actors and actresses, oiled with various preparations to keep themselves from getting sunburned, lay gleaming on the sand, or walked along the edge of the surf, as I once saw Richard Barthelmess do. On a morning, the next-door neighbors appeared, Lilyan Tashman in a startling white bathing suit, her face a polar snowfield of cold cream, and her husband, Edmund Lowe, with his black thread of mustache.

One Sunday morning, John Gilbert took me for a long walk, holding my hand and talking to me in his high, thin voice. Most weekends I was there, one of my father's actor friends, Charles Bickford, would drop by from somewhere to sit on the beach and talk to Daddy in his deep voice.

After he had gone, Daddy said, "Actors are so dumb. You wouldn't believe how dumb they are!"

Mary Barthelmess, a few years older than I, gave me a pair of rose-colored beach pajamas she had outgrown. When I tried them on, I was stung on my rear end by a bee trapped inside the cotton folds. I had learned it was dangerous to complain within my mother's hearing. My hand flew to cover my mouth and hold in my startled cry.

Several weeks earlier, I had murmured to Daddy that I had a toothache. My mother just then entered the room. In a neutral voice she said, "I'll fix that for you." She turned, smiling, to my father. "Would you put her in the rumble seat?" It may have seemed to him that she had nothing in mind but a short drive in the open air, but I heard sounds of distant thunder.

She drove on the steep, curving hills that rose across from Malibu. Through the back window, I saw how rigidly she held her back, how stiff her neck was, as she drove like the wind and I was shaken like a rattle.

The drive lasted twenty minutes or so—the drive lasted forever. When we returned to the beach house, she emerged from the car and stood like a statue for a moment, staring at me in the rumble seat with her great dark eyes, her face stony. "Do you still have a toothache?" she inquired politely. Driving me on the mountain roads had not lessened her rage but intensified it.

One afternoon I found my father slouched in a canvas chair on the "captain's bridge," a bottle of gin on the floor next to his right foot. "Colonel Fear," he called out, in a stupefied voice. I glanced quickly back at the door, thinking someone might be there. No one. "Have you ever met him? Ah, if you'd met him, you'd not forget him," he muttered. Briefly his bloodshot blue eyes came into focus. He saw it was me. "And whose little girl are you?" he inquired, in a comical falsetto voice. When I laughed, he said, "I knew when I took you to the Adirondacks that I'd won you. I licked up a bit of salt I'd spilled on my hand, and you said, 'You're funny,' and that's how I knew."

It was true that he had won me. Part of the time he was an ally, part of the time a betrayer. I was not afraid of him, only of what he might do. One afternoon when he dropped me into the ocean, and I was sputtering as I dog-paddled—though by that time I had overcome my terror to some extent—he asked me whom I'd prefer to be stranded on a desert island with, Vin Lawrence or himself. Perversely, I said, "Vin!" to his bobbing head a few yards away. He laughed, swallowed water, swam to me, and held my arm all the way back to the beach.

Vin Lawrence told me about an evening walking along the beach with my father. He said that earlier they had lifted a few glasses. As they walked, they found themselves treading on hundreds of tiny fish puffing and flopping on the sand. My father threw them back into the ocean, handfuls at a time. The surf flung them up on the beach again. "He was frantic," Vin said. When I grew up, I learned the fish had come to the beach to mate and then to die.

One night, along with an actor, Minor Watson, my father drove us to Venice Amusement Park. The roller coaster's dark coil lifted up from the surface of the black water and flung its length farther into the darkness. Only a few small bulbs hung from a wire, casting a dim light on the narrow tracks. Daddy persuaded me to try the ride. I was reluctant. Still, I stepped after him into one of the open cars where Minor Watson was already sitting, a vague, kindly smile on his face.

We plunged and ascended. I howled to be let off, howled in fright, clutched my father's jacket until, as the track leveled out, the car slowed down before coming to a halt.

Dazed, I stumbled along the pier until I heard my father's voice calling me. I turned around to see Daddy and Minor standing together in front of a glaringly lit shooting gallery, their faces in shadow. I felt I didn't know anyone in the world, and no one knew me.

Daddy picked up a rifle chained to the counter, shot, hit a target, and won a stuffed animal. On our return to Malibu, he drew the car up in front of a sprawling estate in Santa Monica.

"Pal, take this creature to the door," he said, as he handed me the toy, "and give it to anyone who answers the bell. Whoever the hell it is, tell him the bear is for your cousin, Douglas Fairbanks."

The task restored some balance I'd lost on the roller-coaster ride, and I did it willingly. I walked up a long path to the front door and rang an ornate bell. After a while, it was answered by an old man in some sort of costume. He peered down at me and asked, "Yes, miss?"

I handed up the bear and repeated my father's message.

The old man accepted both words and toy and said he'd pass them on to Mr. Fairbanks when he returned from the studio.

The last day I spent at Malibu Beach, Uncle Elwood appeared on the sand wearing a black bathing suit.

I don't know how he had arrived there. I knew he had come to see me. I took his hand and led him across sand warmed by the morning sun and into the foaming surf, urging him on, elatedly, until we were both dog-paddling in the Pacific. He came the next day and then, as far as I knew, returned to Balmville.

Within a month or two of his visit, I too returned to the minister's house on the hill, with whom or how I don't recall.

I thought I might burst with happiness, freed from a year-long curse, as though I were a girl in a fairy tale.

Uncle Elwood told me he had stood on the roof of the old stable to watch the California-bound train make its way north on the east bank of the Hudson River, the train I had been on with Aunt Jessie.

One afternoon I saw a taxi pause at the bottom of the driveway. An elderly woman emerged from the passenger seat.

It had been raining on and off for days. The driveway was impassable for most cars except for Uncle Elwood's doughty old Packard. I watched the woman make her slow way through the rain and mud.

At last she stood in the hall, laughing with what I took to

be embarrassment at her disheveled state, at the mud on her shoes.

"Paulita," she said. My heart sank. She was my Spanish grandmother, come to take me away. Her duties with her Spanish relative in Cuba were lighter; she would not be traveling there every year. At some moment during the grim hours that followed each other like links in a chain drawing me away from Uncle Elwood, she looked at me for a long moment and then said to him, "She is of my blood."

It was far worse than a fairy-tale enchantment. My parting from the minister was an amputation.

Long Island

Once upon a time, there were four brothers, Fermin, Leopold, Frank (also known as Panchito), and Vincent. There was a sister, too, Elsie, youngest of them all. Two of the brothers, Leopold and Vincent, lived with their mother, my grandmother, Candelaria, in a small brick house on Audley Street, in Kew Gardens, Long Island. I went to live there in 1930.

Fermin, the oldest son, was married to Elpidia, a peasant woman born in a small Cuban village. They lived in a section of New York City then known as Spanish Harlem with their two daughters, Isabel and Natalie. Eventually, a third daughter was born, Alicia.

Frank was employed by a pharmaceutical company as a salesman. His work required him to travel in South America, a good market for drugs. In his youth, he had played baseball and had almost made it into the major leagues. He was the most American of his mother's five children, at least externally.

Vincent, small of stature, with no visible waist, kept up his trousers with suspenders. He accompanied singers or violinists on the piano and was sometimes away on tour. Most afternoons he left the brick house swiftly and silently on mysterious errands. When he was home, he practiced the piano all day long, or so it seemed to me.

When Frank dropped in for a visit after months away in Peru or Argentina, Vincent didn't look up from the keyboard until he had completed the piece he was playing. With a sliding glance at his brother, he would say, "Oh. Hello. Frank."

He spoke English with a severe and glacial precision, seeming to bite each word like a coin to test its genuineness before letting it go.

After I had been living on Audley Street a month or so, he followed me into the bathroom one morning. I was sitting on the toilet. He turned on a tap in the sink so the sound of water flowing covered the trickle of my urine. "You see?" he stated grimly. He repeated the two words, providing his own echo.

My father once said mockingly, "Vi-cen-tīc-o plays the ampīc-o . . . and says everything twice." *Two* must have held an eerie numerical spell over Vincent. As well as repeating words twice, he tripped twice every time he climbed a flight of stairs.

Leopold lived on the top floor of the house in a studio-like room with a skylight. A large drawing board tilted at an angle was the first thing I saw when the door opened. At its top was a narrow trench holding several drawing pencils and the razor blades he sharpened them with. Each razor bore a thumbprint-shaped smudge of black powder from the veins of lead that ran through the pencils.

Leopold was an art director at Macfadden Publications. He showed me a photograph of Mr. Macfadden, posing as the world's strongest man in a *True Story* magazine advertisement for a product or an exercise—I forget which—guaranteed to make weaklings strong. He wore bathing trunks that revealed his tanned chest and arms sheathed in muscles that resembled dark taffy. He looked very old—which, Leopold explained, made his muscular development the more remarkable.

Leopold was away on vacation when I arrived at the house on Audley Street. I suffered from piercing earaches in the first few weeks. My grandmother, alarmed by my anguished cries, telephoned the minister for help. When I learned he was coming, my weeping ceased. But I knew, a desperate knowing, that he would stay only a few hours. The earaches diminished in intensity. That time Uncle Elwood visited me in Kew Gardens was the last time I saw him for many years. We wrote each other periodically.

My heart had grown dull. Sorrow, and the changes in my life that were its cause, had worked its desolation upon me.

Leopold changed that. He taught me chess and swung me in the air, and his large-hearted laughter lifted my spirits. When I opened the door to his room, I breathed in the buoyant aroma of the Cuban cigars he smoked. His deep-set dark eyes were like my mother's except for their tenderness of expression. His stride was graceful, wary, and indomitable, like a big cat's.

When Vincent was away and only my grandmother and Leopold were in the house, I rested safely in the present.

But when Vincent returned to Audley Street from his engagements, I stayed outdoors after school. I played with neighborhood children or by myself until it was the hour when Leopold would arrive at the Kew Gardens railroad station. I watched from a living room window as he walked up the narrow cement path, too narrow to accommodate his stride; he stepped off it, now and then, onto patches of rusty-looking grass on either side.

I would run to the hall in time to see him greet his mother and bend down to kiss her cheek—none of the other brothers kissed her—and after I'd waited awhile, I'd go upstairs and knock on his door. He would open it and smile down at me.

On sunny weekends, his studio, as he called it, was radiant with light. It was a different world from the bleak floor below. I slept in the same bed with my grandmother if Vincent was home. He always took my small room and bed.

"Have the sheets been changed?" he'd call out in the hall, without troubling to see if there was anyone within range to hear him. I could sense his rage, suddenly flaring up like a banked fire.

Once in a great while, Fermin visited. The fire of his rage was *not* banked. He maintained a grim silence around us, breaking it only to mutter furiously into my grandmother's ear. I knew she felt his heated breath. While she listened, her expression was one of strained submission, not so much a response to what he was telling her as the habitual mode of her being.

She had been born in northern Spain. After a sea voyage to Cuba, she was married to my grandfather, the owner of a sugar plantation, Cienegita. The marriage had been arranged by her parents with the advice of their cousin, Luisa Ponvert, owner of Olmiguero, a neighboring plantation.

Widowed at an early age, my grandmother came to the United States with her five children soon after the end of the Spanish-American War. During its last days, Cienegita was burned to the ground by what she described as a band of carpetbaggers, who left intact only the machinery for boiling the sugarcane.

Her father offered her $5,000, a very large sum in those days, to return to Spain. But she wanted to live in the country her husband had loved and often visited on plantation business.

She was sixteen when she first arrived in Havana. One afternoon, before meeting her bridegroom, she told me she had stepped onto the balcony of the house in Havana where she was staying temporarily with family friends. She was on the fourth floor, and to see the street more clearly she knelt down, pushed her head through two bars of the balcony's railing, and then couldn't withdraw it. A crowd gathered on the street. Some people laughed; some looked worried. Eventually she was freed from the grille, not much the worse for wear. The crowd had distracted her from her own plight and kept her amused and interested.

When my mother was nineteen, she gave birth to me. At some point during her pregnancy, she also went to the house on Audley Street, and my father with her. But he and Leopold, whom he'd met in the navy during the early months of U.S. involvement in the war in 1917, left at once to board a tramp steamer bound for South America. As he left the house, my mother raced after him and hurled a bottle of sauce at his back. It missed, he told me, and he and Leopold ran off to sea like careless, triumphant boys.

At a port in some Central American country, they disembarked and went to a hotel where my uncle smilingly, languidly, remarked that he didn't feel like translating that day. He sat down in a handy chair and lit a cigar, listening with the air of a remote linguistic connoisseur to the struggle of a local fellow, who claimed to be bilingual, to comprehend and convert to Spanish my father's questions about the cost of room and meals and then to turn the clerk's answers into a dim semblance of English.

I went to Public School 99, a small elementary school that stood next to a large cemetery, which I explored in the afternoons after school. I read headstones as if they were the beginnings and ends of stories; death was inconceivable to me except for those moments at night when I awoke and listened to the beating of my heart. Some knowledge, not of the heart or of the mind, perhaps of the cells, informed me that one day that pulsation would cease.

During the year on Audley Street, one night when I was within a blink of sleep, the door to my little room opened. At first I thought it was Vincent come to claim my bed, but it was my father.

I had not seen him for two years. He didn't turn on the light but left the door ajar, so that the hall light fell across the bedclothes, my upward struggling self, and his face. He spoke just above a whisper, perhaps not to wake me completely, but I was fully awake and full of longing and a prescient sense of loss. He could not have stayed for more than twenty minutes —he had dropped by to visit Leopold—and me, of course— but he assured me in the beautiful rumble of his voice that he would see me "very, very, very soon" and rose from the edge of the bed and left.

I was distraught for hours. I felt a queasy emptiness in my stomach as I lay there in the dark. When I awoke in the morning, it seemed my father had visited me in a dream.

At P.S. 99, the first class of the day was arithmetic, taught by Mrs. Goldberg. One morning she introduced us to banking, providing each of us with a facsimile of a blank check. After we had worked a few minutes, she called upon me to read what I had written.

"Pay to the order of my father—" I began. My classmates howled with exaggerated laughter and dropped their books on the floor. Mrs. Goldberg looked at me humorously and asked what my father's name was. But I was mute, unable to answer. Mrs. Goldberg was not a torturer. She let me sit down and called on another child.

But we were torturers. There were two vulnerable teachers, Miss Grady and Miss Banta. Miss Grady was rumored to have a relative on the school board who had gotten her her position. She had a large beauty spot that changed position frequently on her old apple of a face. Once she kept me after class and pleaded with me—reasonably, I think—to behave in class and stop making funny faces in the back row where I sat. She said she was appealing to my evident intelligence. I sensed weakness. Then suddenly I saw her, an elderly large woman with brown hair turning gray caught up in a loose bun at the back of her head, sitting slumped in the teacher's chair, pitied no doubt by her relative on the school board and for a brief instant by me. I bowed my head too full of the sense of her to speak, and left the classroom.

Miss Banta taught art. A classmate of mine and I wrote her notes pretending to be from an anonymous suitor. We found her telephone number and called her up in the late afternoon, imitating, successfully we thought, male voices. One day after class, she asked us to stay.

"I want this to stop," she said calmly, almost thoughtfully. "It's gone far enough." No weakness there!

Our spelling teacher, a heavily freckled, pinched-looking woman whose name I can't recall, came into the classroom one day with a sanitary pad poking up from her gaping pocketbook. The girls sat frozen. A few boys hooted. None of us, I think, had anything but a faint idea of the use of that contrivance of cotton and gauze. It had to do with being "grown up." It had to do with sexual life.

The girls were humiliated by the sight of it. Yet it had a kind of dark glamour. Full of a shadowy foreknowledge, we looked at the teacher with scorn. She had a careless, abstracted manner, and when she spoke to the class, she stared over our heads to the wall behind us.

On Fridays, the whole school, students and teachers, marched into the auditorium, where a radio had been rigged up to an amplifying system, and we heard Walter Damrosch's *Concerts for Children*.

"Now, children," Mr. Damrosch would begin; then he would sing, unmelodically:

> *"This is—the sym-pho-ny*
> *that Schubert wrote and never fi-nished."*

It made an indelible impression on my brain, and when I hear that symphony today, I still sing Damrosch's note-matching words.

On Friday afternoons I went to the public library, where as

often as not I would take out a book by Frank Baum, one of a series about an imaginary country named Oz. One day, a set of *The Books of Knowledge* turned up in the Audley Street house, bought for me, I suspect, by Leopold.

Subjects were alphabetically arranged, and when I looked up one thing, the definition and information in it led me to other things. Looking through the volumes, pausing to read about beetles or Paris or aviation, was like continuing the tales begun in the *National Geographics* I had discovered in Uncle Elwood's attic—pictures and words about life and its astonishments. The books in their red bindings breathed for me a kind of intimacy.

One morning my grandmother made me a different breakfast from the usual toast and cereal. She minced garlic and spread it on a slice of bread that had been soaked in olive oil. A memory stirred—something about Elsie. My arrival at school was greeted by my classmates with cries of mock disgust, hands outstretched to keep me at a distance.

I was the foreigner in a school population made up largely of children from working-class Irish Catholic families. The final damning evidence of my foreignness was my grandmother herself, when she appeared in school on those days set aside for parents to visit classes.

She did not resemble any other mother. She was older, of course. And she had a thick Spanish accent. As I looked at her sitting at a child's desk, a hairpin worked itself loose from the bun she wore and fell onto the desktop. Her hair was not like the permanent-waved hair of some of the mothers. But I loved the bread soaked in oil and covered with garlic, and I didn't give it up once I'd tasted it.

Prejudice has its own headaches. I was a puzzle to my classmates. I was fair-haired and might have been taken for a Scandinavian. One branch of my relatives in southern Spain was descended from the emirate of Granada. What would the children have done if they had learned I had Arab ancestors from North Africa?

As it was, they didn't know what to think of me. They settled on halfway measures, tormenting me from time to time, becoming friendly when they forgot—as children did in those days—exactly what they were tormenting me about. But then their attention was diverted from me by the arrival of two boys, also "foreigners," an Armenian and a French-Canadian whose accent was as thick as my grandmother's. The three of us contrived a small country of our own.

In a sense, garlic saved me, confirming my position as an outsider and preventing me from absorbing any unselfquestioning assumptions about national or personal superiority.

Time deceives memory. My circumstances seemed to have changed overnight, but it must have happened over months, slowly.

The brick house on Audley Street was sold. My grandmother and I moved into the first of two apartments in a building on Metropolitan Avenue on the ever-widening outskirts of Kew Gardens. Vincent disappeared. Frank was traveling in South America. Leopold moved into an apartment in New York City. I learned a new, longer way to walk to P.S. 99, but I used it only for a few months.

One morning before I set off for school, my grandmother told me that in a few days she and I were going to Cuba to spend a year or so on a sugar plantation owned by a cousin of ours whom I was to address as "Tía Luisa."

I didn't know where Cuba was, but I found it in a school atlas, a green lizard lying athwart a blue sea.

Cuba

My grandmother and I left Kew Gardens early one morning toward the end of 1931. We took the Long Island Rail Road to Pennsylvania Station in New York City, and as we carried our suitcases along the side of another train, nearly hidden by a rolling cocoon of steam, she told me that Tía Luisa owned the last car.

How could one person *own* a railroad car?

An elderly man hurried toward us. "Good morning, Señora de Sola," he said, bowing slightly. "Let me take your luggage." He looked down at me and smiled.

Before he boarded a car with our suitcases, I glimpsed his pale blue eyes and white hair. My grandmother said his name was Prince and he was an English butler who was the head of Tía Luisa's staff of servants. Among them, she told me, were Tía Luisa's own seamstress, known as La Gallega to the staff because she had been born in Galicia, Spain, and her personal physician, Dr. Babito.

I thought to myself that Prince's smile was a sign that he forgave us for being poor.

We stepped onto the platform. The entrance to the private car was partly screened by pots of palm trees reaching to the ceiling. Beyond them in a regal armchair dozed a small elderly woman. Her eyebrows were like black caterpillars that had come to a halt on her forehead, and her small bejeweled hands lay crumpled in her lap.

Servants were moving about silently in the car. The carpet muffled the sounds of their footsteps as they arranged things in drawers.

They slept in berths in another car, as I did. My grandmother spent the nights with Tía Luisa in a bedroom at the end of the private car. I heard later from La Gallega that on very hot afternoons in central Olmiguero, on the plantation she owned, Tía Luisa would rise from her siesta, creep to an open window, and shout for the officer, long dead, she had loved in her youth but not married, to present himself: *"¡Mi coronel! ¡Mi coronel! ¡Adelante!"*

Despite these fits of madness, she was sane enough to run the plantation profitably with the help of her surviving son, Eli. Her younger son, a pilot in the World War, had been shot down. When I heard about him and his fate, I envisioned him descending to the earth gripping a spiraling rope of fire.

A smell pervaded the private car that might have come from the palms or the earth they were rooted in, or something else in the atmosphere, I thought later: a ripe, green, warm smell from Cuba itself.

During the first month I spent in Olmiguero, I hurried out of bed as soon as I awoke in the mornings. I was mad to begin the day, its glowing yellow light shining through the slats of the wood shutters on the windows of a room near the servants' quarters I shared with my grandmother. She might come to bed long after dark, after Tía Luisa dismissed her. Often she wasn't dismissed, and I slept alone.

In the vast kitchen where I ate fruit standing at a counter, servants buzzed and swarmed, halting for a few seconds in the preparation of breakfast trays to drink from their own cups of *café con leche*. They were harried by the nearly constant jangling of the bells in an open box affixed to the wall with numbers corresponding to the bedrooms of the waking household. I knew better than to try at such times to get the attention of Emilio, a cook and my friend in the kitchen, comical, plump, and good-natured. He and La Gallega, the seamstress, kept an eye on my comings and goings. But not on all of them, especially in the mornings when they were so busy.

I usually went to the orchard, where oranges and grapefruit and bananas ripened on short thick-trunked trees. Scattered among them, bearing fruit I didn't recognize, were thin tall trees that loomed over the orchard. Beyond them was a sea of sugarcane. The smell I had noticed on the train was powerfully present everywhere I went in Olmiguero.

I spent hours in the vast formal garden. Gravel-covered paths wound among beds and hills of flowers. I saw Tía Luisa being pushed among them in a wheelchair by Prince now and then. She had a sulky, pettish expression on her face. Sometimes she was asleep.

At the north side of the garden, dividing it from wild unkept land where pigs rooted and rolled, were two large cages, one filled with brilliantly feathered birds, the other with thin black and white monkeys that swung to and fro through the air from the branches of a dead tree. Sitting below them among rinds and cores of fruit was a cranky-looking fat gray monkey. His eyes blinked rapidly when I came near. I gave the animals my lunches—rice and beans, fried and salted disks of banana, a slab of meat—especially when the day was intensely hot and such big meals upset my stomach.

At first I had felt exhilarated by freedom. But soon I began to be lonely. There was no one who said my name for hours at a time.

Three wooden steps descended to the ground from the back door of the kitchen. I took them at a jump. One morning I found a stone-faced man in a suit waiting near the steps. "*Vamos a la escuela,*" he said, in a spiritless voice, walking a few steps, looking back to see that I was following him. I did, kicking up fans of dust, wondering if I'd find a friend in the school where he was leading me.

We left the garden and Tía Luisa's grand house, passing the

ingenio de azúcar, the sugar refinery, from which issued a great throbbing like a monstrous heart. The man abruptly stopped. He said, '"*Aquí*." We had arrived at the chapel, where I had been many times before, dreaming through masses. As soon as we entered, he knelt. I heard his knee creak as he rose after crossing himself furtively. He accompanied me as far as the altar. Nearby was a black curtain he drew aside to reveal a closed door. I heard the voices of children.

For a moment, I was afraid. I turned to my guide but he was walking, nearly running, up the aisle toward the entrance.

I opened the door to a large square room with a blackboard at one end nearly covered by a ragged cloth map of the world, hanging unevenly, the kind of map that can be lowered or raised by two cords.

They must have heard earlier that I was coming to the school. Everyone was smiling, calling my name, nine students and their teacher, Señora García.

In the fourth grade at P.S. 99, on Long Island, a slam book was handed around the class, a student's name at the top of each page, below it a blank space where you could write, anonymously, your most damning thoughts. The written names seemed to shiver in the glare and coldness of the cruel judgments below. The slam book had appeared mysteriously in the third or fourth week of October. Someone had written below my name, *She stays up all night thinking of things to write and say the next day*. I puzzled over the handwriting and the meaning, but of course it was partly true.

The children in Señora García's classroom were of different ages, the oldest around twelve, the youngest close to my age. I don't know how she was able to teach children of such varied ages in one classroom but she managed to do so. At times, still older children turned up in class, only to be absent the next day or the next week. I heard they worked in the cane fields.

I began to be glad that there was no one person looking after me. I soon discovered a way to Señora García's house. It was a real house, larger than the neighboring houses, or *bohíos*, as they were called by the families who lived in them. Unlike the Señora's, the bohíos were raised several feet above the ground on stilts. Underneath them chickens scratched and clucked incessantly.

The Señora's kitchen was clean; a doorway was covered with a beaded curtain and led to a second room, where I glimpsed a bed. No one who worked for the plantation had inside lavatories as far as I knew, not even the Garcías, and few had two rooms as they did.

The kitchen was a place to meet other children, and we were made welcome by la Señora unless her husband was home. Her kitchen was equipped with a sink and a water tap. She heated water in a kettle on the stove many times over to fill a movable tin tub, where each of us had a bath. After la Señora had put up my hair in paper twists so it would be curly for a few hours, we were ready for our *paseo*, a walk through the plantation.

We passed freight cars loaded with cut cane waiting for the engine that drew them to the mill, where the cane was crushed and the resulting liquid boiled in vast iron vats over huge fires. We walked through fields of growing cane until we came to open countryside. On the bank of a small pond surrounded by wild palms and tall straggling grass, a group of boys was gathered. They all had on the big-brimmed straw hats the grown-up men wore. Their voices, their laughter, rang out in the heat-stilled afternoon. They had been let off their work in the cane fields. I knew some of them. I had played baseball with the younger boys four or five times. Their fathers had called me *"la ciclón de Olmiguero"* and laughed as they said it, but I sensed reproach in their attitude. Yet in time, as the shock wore off of seeing me play baseball, so did the nickname of cyclone. I suppose they forgave me because I was a child and from *el norte*, as they referred to the United States. I couldn't be expected to know their rules of conduct.

I had seen the older boys gathered around that same pond, tossing stones at a flock of tiny white owls sheltering in a palm tree, blinded by daylight. One was hit and fell straight into the pond, a ball of white feathers tinged with blood. "No!" I cried out, but they paid me no attention, except for one who looked at me with a trace of indignation, as though I'd interrupted a ritual.

In the latter part of the day, a breeze would spring up and rustle among palm fronds and grassy fields, blowing the temporary curls off of my forehead. I was always stirred by the cooling of the day.

When the weather changed and the heat intensified, torrents of rain fell for two or three hours every afternoon. The meetings with other children in the García kitchen continued. We listened to records played on a phonograph, songs and dances that were popular in Havana. One of us would wind the arm of the phonograph when the record ended.

During a rare hailstorm, I and my friends ran shrieking with excitement onto the cracked cement of a tennis court, unused for years ever since Tía Luisa's son had grown too old to play the game.

I went home before dark. My supper awaited me on a tray in the kitchen. The servants were rushing about as they prepared dinner for Tía Luisa, Eli Ponvert, my grandmother, and themselves.

La Gallega stopped to pat my shoulder, and Emilio winked at me as they went about their tasks, Emilio carrying trays of covered platters on his way to the dining room, the seamstress on her feet, hastily mending a tear in a linen napkin. Later, I would go to my bedroom, tiptoeing along the hallway like a shadow.

I had begun to belong to the plantation but not to the people in the grand house—who had not, in any case, asked for me. It was in the evenings that I most missed the minister—and books.

* * *

I heard often from Uncle Elwood. But one time he didn't write for weeks. When a black-bordered envelope arrived for me, I knew it contained the news of the death of his mother, Emily Corning.

One Sunday I went with my grandmother to the chapel. A visiting priest was holding a special mass to pray for the return of Tía Luisa's health and sanity. It was extremely hot; the heat had a sound, the rustle of the palmetto fans with which people tried to cool their faces. We rose to recite the stations of the cross. I didn't know the words so I muttered gibberish. Suddenly, I felt queasy and lightheaded.

The congregation, stupefied by heat and their own droning, didn't notice that I had fainted in the aisle. When I came to, they were still praying, and I crawled to the chapel entrance. A man was passing on the road, pushing a wheelbarrow. He looked at me and said, "Get into my ambulance," and I crawled into it. He took me to the wooden building where the plantation doctor had his office.

The doctor laughed as he lifted me out of the wheelbarrow. He was short and fat and elderly, a specialist, I had been told, in machete cuts and internal parasites. His small office smelled agreeably of cigar smoke. I rested on a couch while he scribbled at his desk. I must have fallen asleep. No one was in the office when I woke. I ran all the way home, got there in time for my lunch, and fed it to the monkeys.

* * *

My grandmother and I traveled to Cienfuegos, a port town on the Caribbean, just south of the plantation. We had an appointment with a doctor. In the kitchen, I had been complaining about pains in my stomach after Emilio found me feeding the monkeys. The news had reached my grandmother. It was the first time we'd been together in weeks, except at night when we were both sleeping. I asked her what she did for Tía Luisa.

She said she was her companion. I had seen that word in stories. One went on one's travels with a companion. Later, I discovered she was paid for it, $200 a month, which continued for years, even after Tía Luisa was dead. I knew she was a kind of servant to the old woman. Everyone on the plantation was a servant, except Tía Luisa and her son.

The new doctor's office was filled with instruments of which I could see he was proud. He began nearly every sentence with, "What we have here is a great advance in medical science, a fluoroscope"—or a special X-ray machine, or an implement to be used in surgery. I stood in front of the fluoroscope, a glass oyster-colored screen where he could peer at my innards. "Nervous indigestion," he pronounced.

On the train returning to Santa Clara, the plantation's district, my grandmother sighed and said my mother's perpetual stomach troubles had begun with nervous indigestion. Ever since I had lived with her, I had heard about Elsie's gut. I was instantly haunted as always by my grandmother's stories—and her infrequent advice such as, "If you don't dry between your toes after bathing, you'll bring on an attack of appendicitis." One of her stories from the time she lived on my grandfather's plantation, Cienegita, was about a tapeworm excreted into a toilet by one of the maids. The tapeworm was wound around and around, filling up all the space. Every time she spoke of it, the worm lengthened.

A dwarf lived and worked in Olmiguero. When I first saw him, I thought he was a misshapen child. Upon closer inspection, I realized he was an elderly man. He was sweet-natured and amiable, and let us all touch the hump on his back as we said "*Enano*" for good luck.

One evening, a movie was shown in the Olmiguero community hall. I was sent to see it by my grandmother, accompanied by the same man who had taken me to the chapel to attend school. He was as silent as he had been that day. When we came to the hall, he left me at the entrance, muttering he would return to get me when the movie was over.

The interior was filled up with scissor-legged wooden chairs upon which were sitting what seemed like the entire population of Olmiguero, even the dwarf. There was an air of great expectation among people. Something rare, something out of the ordinary, was about to happen.

Words suddenly appeared on a screen: THE WAY OF ALL FLESH. I looked back at the ray of dusty lunar light that threw the image above our heads to the screen. The star of the movie was Emil Jannings.

The story begins. It is Christmas. A happy family circles a decorated tree. They live in a small happy town. The father is sent to the big city by his company. The first night, he goes into a bar, orders a nonalcoholic drink. A powerful drug is slipped into his glass. He passes out, comes to, finds himself lying across railroad tracks. A corpse lies a few feet away. He's killed a man! What horror! A shattered creature, he staggers up a bank. Every neon sign turns into MURDERER! or KILLER! Years pass. His circumstances are so reduced, he is forced to gather trash in a public park. His beard is long and white.

It is winter again. He makes his way on foot to the little town, finds the house he once lived in, looks through a frosty window at his family, gathered for another Christmas. His children are now grown up, although his wife hasn't aged at all.

I was struck down by the movie, so overcome with sorrow at the old man's plight, I sobbed all the way to the house. I couldn't spare a glance at the man who accompanied me, keeping his distance across the road, and whom I'd found waiting for me outside the hall, hunched over, looking down at the ground.

One afternoon after the rainy season, I was on my way to Señora García's house. I was surprised to see cane cutters gathered in groups on the dirt road, agitated, angry, some of them gesturing with clenched hands at the sky.

That day, Señora García was not her usual welcoming self. Her husband was home, a tall thin man in a suit with a thatch of gray hair over a stern face. By then I knew he worked in the plantation's administration office.

There were no children in the kitchen; the tin tub was resting on its side in a corner. I was bewildered and apprehensive. Señora García glanced at me for a second, gave me a hurried smile, turned to her husband, and they went on with their conversation in low voices.

I left the house and made my way past the cane-filled freight cars, the chapel, the mill, to the stone portico of the big house. I rarely entered the house by the front doors. A dozen rocking chairs were lined up along the portico, empty, seeming to wait. I went down a corridor to the kitchen and found the servants sitting at a big table, their heads bent, talking to each other in alarmed voices. I waved at Emilio, who looked at me without seeing me. Then he started. "Ay! Paulita!"

I knew an event was forming itself as black clouds form in a menacing sky. When my grandmother came to bed that night, I asked her what was happening. She answered by saying that we were all returning to Havana in a day or so.

Dr. Babito, my grandmother, and I stayed with Tía Luisa at the Hotel Nacional in Havana. The servants were quartered in smaller hotels in the city and had to rise early in the morning to get to the hotel before my ancient cousin waked.

My grandmother was always with her, while I wandered

along the corridors and the huge lobby. I was under the illusion that the hotel staff were now my caretakers, and that the permission of the bell captain was required before I could use the swimming pool in the gardens.

"May I use the pool today?" I would ask him. He would close his eyes, appear to ponder, then arrive at a decision. "Yes, but only this morning," he would answer, in a tone of reluctant judiciousness.

There were American tourists staying at the hotel, and one descended in the elevator with me. He leaned against the elevator paneling, cushioning himself with both hands.

"You have such honest gray eyes," he commented.

"My eyes are blue," I replied, not cheekily, only to set the record straight.

He bent forward to look at me more closely. "So they are," he said.

When the elevator reached the lobby and the two of us walked out of it, several hotel employees sprang forward.

"Meester Keaton!" they exclaimed in unison. The bell captain whispered to me, "El Señor Buster Keaton," but the name meant nothing to me.

"Can I swim today?" I asked him.

He nodded, his attention on Meester Keaton. I changed into my bathing suit in a small house beside the pool, a blue oblong of glittering water. I dog-paddled about.

On a morning a few days later, the bell captain said a resounding "No!" to my usual question.

I was startled and disappointed. He must have noticed because he added, more softly, "The revolution began today."

The afternoon of the same day, young men came to the Hotel Nacional and hurled stones at some of the windows. I heard sporadic shooting. A day or so later, we embarked on a ship bound for Florida.

When we arrived in New York City, Tía Luisa, in the care of Dr. Babito and Prince, was driven to the Plaza Hotel, where she kept a suite, using it two weeks of the year. That same week my grandmother said that the president of Cuba, Gerardo Machado, had been overthrown. It was 1933. I was ten years old.

New York City

My grandmother and I boarded a Long Island train and were back in Kew Gardens after an absence of more than sixteen months.

Our suitcases on the floor beside our feet, we stared into the one-room apartment we had returned to, and for which my grandmother had paid rent for so many months. Dust covered everything. There was a stale smell in the air.

I began to choke. In a strangled voice, I managed to say, "It's so small . . . ."

She took a step into the room. A high counter divided the living-sleeping area from the kitchen and dinette. We unpacked and put our things away in silence.

A few weeks later, my Uncle Fermin's wife, Elpidia, came to stay for several days. She took my place alongside my grandmother in the Murphy pull-down bed that each night emerged like a mastodon from the closet where it lived. I slept in the bathtub while she was there, placing a heavy blanket on the porcelain and a hard cushion from the sofa for my head.

I don't know why Elpidia came but I recall how relieved I was to go off to P.S. 99 in the mornings and escape the sounds of her deep sighs and the refrain that accompanied them, "*¡Ay, Dios! Qué me ayuda!*" Her face was always damp with recently shed tears. I tried to learn their cause, but her conversations in the kitchen with my grandmother ended as soon as I entered the dinette, and the wall muffled their words.

When she left, I returned to my side of the bed.

I slipped into P.S. 99 as though I'd only been absent one afternoon. There were new students, among them two boys. One was tall and horse-faced and cracked his knuckles constantly. The other was blond-haired, tall but slender, whom I thought beautiful. He wore white shirts open at the collar, and he had a stern, cool expression on his face. I thought of a boy alone on a mountaintop, looking down on the world. He erased Freddie Harrison of Balmville from memory and took his place for nearly a decade. But for a long time, he didn't give me a tumble.

One afternoon he asked me for the time. I glanced at the Mickey Mouse watch my grandmother had given me and told him. He said, "That's just a cheap boy's watch."

I went to the movies every Saturday afternoon. My friends and I exchanged the sepia-colored photographs of movie stars we cut out of magazines. There was little as satisfying as settling down on the floor in the bedrooms of other girls, a heap of magazines nearby and scissors close at hand.

One stormy night I was visiting a friend who lived in another apartment house. Her older sister came in, her hair tousled by the wind and damp from the rain, saying in an exuberant voice, "It feels like the end of the world outside!" These words struck me as original, profound, and elegant. I wished I had said them.

I was the recipient of a paper sack stuffed with discarded clothes from my cousin Natalie, the daughter of Fermin and Elpidia. Stained slips, wool stockings worn thin at the heels, garter belts with flaccid suspenders, and ragged brassieres were all wound around each other like sleeping snakes. At the bottom of the sack was a print dress made of some slippery material—rayon, perhaps. It had a ropelike belt with tasseled ends that looped twice around my waist. I wore it to school, though it was far too large, and its pattern of large, ugly green flowers made it, somehow, unseemly.

Natalie, several years older than I, lived in a railroad flat with her parents, a grown-up sister, a younger one, and a yellow mongrel dog that bit everyone who came to the flat—or threatened to—except her father.

My grandmother and I made periodic visits to their flat in Spanish Harlem. It was a long journey from Kew Gardens on the new subway. My apprehension deepened as we neared the station in the city where we got off. Would Uncle Fermin be at home wearing a hat that hid his eyes? His skin was so white, his nose so like the blade of a knife.

On those long-ago Saturdays, when one of us managed to scrape up enough money for tickets, Natalie and I would spend afternoons at the Bluebird movie house on Broadway and, I think, 158th Street. Cartoons preceded the feature film, along with a serial, *The Invisible Man*, and were greeted by bursts of wild applause. Along with Olive Oyl and her long narrow feet and tiny head, I especially recollect Mickey Mouse, thin and worried-looking in those days, as if he'd just eluded a laboratory technician's grasp, not as he looks today—plump, smug, and bourgeois.

And what movies we saw! All the actors and actresses whose photographs I collected, with their look of eternity! Their radiance, their eyes, their faces, their voices, the suavity of their movements! Their clothes! Even in prison movies, the stars shone in their prison clothes as if tailors had accompanied them in their downfall.

In the Bluebird, it was as though a woman sang stories larger than lives, about fate and love and evil enacted in shadowed rooms and wild landscapes I couldn't enter, only glimpse from where I sat, rapt.

Some Saturdays, as we returned to the tenement where Natalie lived, we heard thumping and could feel through the soles of our feet the vibrations from my uncle's radio, all the way down from the fifth floor to the sidewalk where we had halted. On Natalie's face would appear a distressed, complicit smile, as though she held herself responsible for the noise.

It was not an ordinary radio. My uncle had built a plywood screen that covered the two narrow windows of the tiny parlor at the front of the flat, had fastened all the radio components to it in some way, and added two loudspeakers. Whenever he was in the flat, he turned up the volume as high as it would go.

The room felt ominous, as though something inhabited it that would, in the end, bring down the entire building. In summer, what breezes made their way up the street from the Hudson River a few long blocks away, were shut out by the plywood screen; in winter, wind and cold leaked in around its edges. My uncle sat in the only armchair in the room, wearing his coat and hat whatever the weather, except on the hottest days of summer, submerged in the uproar as though stupefied by it, the yellow dog at his feet growling, no doubt in baffled protest.

Neighbors stopped at the local police station to complain—only a very few tenants had telephones in those days—but the police never came. My grandmother would retire to one of the cell-like bedrooms, with its poverty-green paint on the walls, and lie on a narrow bed, one arm flung across her eyes and brow.

Elpidia had been born in Palmyra, a hamlet in Cuba, a few miles from my grandfather's plantation. Fermin had run off with her, I was told by my grandmother—in a bland tone of voice that seemed to attach neither blame nor responsibility to him—to protest his engagement to the daughter of a neighboring plantation owner, an arrangement made by his father when Fermin was only a bad-tempered boy.

I puzzled over Elpidia's reasons for marrying him. Perhaps she had been carried away by movie love or worship of some sort. Whatever it had been, she had come with him to the United States, *el norte*.

To escape the fearsome radio racket as much as I could, I used to go to the kitchen to watch Elpidia iron on a spindly board that resembled a grasshopper. Grimly, as though she were trying to kill it, she struck at it with a small black iron she had heated on the stove. Whatever garments were spread on the board's surface often bore scorch marks.

On other days of our visits to the flat, I would find my aunt by marriage slumped on a stool drawn up to the kitchen sink, weeping intermittently and silently, one hand supporting her chin as she stared down at the cockroaches that came and went with their hideous broken speed, now a pause, now a rush.

I don't recall her wearing anything but a faded, stained brown cotton housedress. Her breasts looked like poorly stuffed small pillows. In one of them her death began. She developed cancer before her forty-fifth birthday, and after months of suffering, during which Fermin finally found work in the city sanitation department, she died of it.

In Olmiguero, I had learned to speak Spanish. Because of my grandmother's resistance, or inability, to learn much

English—even after decades of living in the United States, she spoke with a thick accent—I now spoke Spanish to her.

One late-winter afternoon, when it had grown dark around four, I walked into the kitchen, halted a few feet from Elpidia, and asked her why she cried so much.

"*No se, mi hija,*" she answered, turning her kindly, utterly miserable face to me. "*No se.*" I don't know, my daughter, I don't know.

My grandmother took me to the theater to see a play she thought I'd like. As the long plum-velvet curtains drew apart, my breath quickened. But the play seemed foolish. It concerned a clownish high school student who was discovered to have made some unflattering cartoons of the principal and his staff. The audience roared with laughter when the cartoonist was sent to the principal's office, where he stood, accused, sobbing in a manifestly fraudulent manner. From the seat next to me, I heard a sound of muted weeping.

A small dark-haired boy sat there, crutches drawn up beside him, one of his legs in an elaborate brace. His cheeks gleamed wetly in the light from the stage.

During the first intermission, I asked my grandmother why the boy wore the brace and used crutches. She guessed, she said, that he'd had infantile paralysis.

I realized that there wasn't only one way to view the world outside.

* * *

My grandmother told me a story about her father. When she was my age, she had taken a walk with him on one of the broad streets in Barcelona called a *rambla*. He was counting aloud. She asked him what he was counting.

"Priests," he said gravely.

A boy named Jay lived in the apartment house. His mother, a huge woman, came to visit my grandmother and sat on a kitchen stool, one buttock on it, the other appearing to float in midair. She was forceful and serene and seemed to want to take over our lives—but with the best of intentions.

One morning Jay pelted me with snowballs. He was a year or two older than I was. I stood with my back against an apartment house wall, a living target. I reported the incident to my grandmother, who passed on the news to Jay's mother. "Why didn't you pelt him back?" she asked. "Then he won't play with me anymore," I said. She looked up at the ceiling pensively. "I see," she said, as if she'd seen more than I intended. That was her way.

That same year I often sat on the gray cement stairs of the rear service stairway and read stories to whatever children I had managed to collect, sometimes as many as four. After a few moments, my listeners began to wander away.

I read them fairy tales and *Gulliver's Travels*. When I began *Treasure Island*, I lost them all during the opening pages of Robert Louis Stevenson's tale. When I looked up, I found I was the only remaining listener.

I made a friend, Bernice, after I returned from Cuba. Bernice and I had two enemies in our class, Janet and Georgina. Georgina had little bosoms like knuckles poking through the pink or baby-blue sweaters she wore to class. Both girls had small skulls covered with tightly permed hair. They smirked at us and muttered what we took to be insults, their heads inclined toward each other, their hands held like scoops over their mouths.

With Bernice I rode the new subway, which had opened a Metropolitan Avenue station. A clerk in the toll booth, handing me my change for a quarter, said, "Here you go, Jean Harlow."

We went into the city to Radio City Music Hall because Bunny, as I called her, had a crush on a drummer in the live orchestra who looked like an actor of the time, Jack Haley.

She didn't care what movie was being shown or what the Rockettes might do. I didn't really love him, but I pretended to, and it was thrilling when the entire orchestra rose up from the pit, playing their instruments.

We usually got seats in the front row at the far right of the huge theater. After we'd been there three or four times, he seemed to recognize us. He smiled in our direction in a way I thought was extremely oily. But Bernice was enchanted by his shadowed features and black hair rising from the pit by degrees, and the way he kept his eyes on her when he wasn't playing.

* * *

The boy I loved was a sphinx. His inscrutability was part of his charm for me. I wrote a detailed description of his looks as if I were drawing a topographical map of love, and then what I had to guess at, his inner life. While I was writing it in the dinette of our apartment late one evening, I was flooded with a kind of miserable happiness. He was always in my consciousness, more than he was, less than he was. Some years after, in early 1939, I visited my grandmother. On impulse I telephoned him. We made a date to meet and go to Flushing Meadows, where the World's Fair was being held.

Harry James and his orchestra played, and we danced. We spent a good deal of time looking at an exhibit of a cloaked and peculiar car, the work of Salvador Dalí.

We stayed late at the fair. We found a bench where he rested his head on my lap. I looked down at him. In the dim light, his face was marmoreal, beyond mortal concerns. I heard later that he'd become involved with a tarty girl I knew slightly. She had breasts like little volcanoes and always wore a knowing smile on her *jolielaide* face.

My parents returned from Europe after a sojourn of three or four years, when I was eleven. They slid into my sight standing on the deck of a small passenger ship out of Marseille that docked in New York City on the Hudson River alongside a cavernous shed. They were returning home after their adventures, the most recent being their flight a few weeks earlier from the Balearic Island of Ibiza during the early days of the Spanish Civil War.

My mother had draped a polo coat over her shoulders—I suppose because it was a cool spring day—and she smiled down at my grandmother and me as we waited in the shadowed darkness of the shed. Sunlight fell in daggers through holes in the roof high above us.

It had been years since I'd seen them. They were as handsome as movie stars. Smoke trailed like a festive streamer from the cigarette my mother held between two fingers of her right hand. When she realized we'd spotted her, she waved once and her head was momentarily wreathed in smoke. The gangplank was lowered thunderously across the abyss between the deck and the pier. Passengers began to trickle across it. Suddenly my parents were standing before us, a steamer trunk like a third presence between them. I knew that trunk; I'd seen it in Provincetown years earlier.

"Hello . . . hello . . . hello," they called to us, as if we were far away. They pointed out their luggage for porters, speaking to my grandmother and me in voices that were deep, melodious—not everyday voices like those I heard in Kew Gardens, but of an unbroken suavity, as though they'd memorized whole pages written for them on this occasion of their homecoming.

They spoke of shipboard life; about a cave in Ibiza outside of which my father had crouched for hours—embarrassed by a fit of claustrophobia that had paralyzed him not two feet from the entrance, while my mother hid inside along with other refugees—before escaping the next day to the ship that carried them to Marseille; about the fact, ruefully acknowledged by both of them with charming smiles, that no troops from either side especially wanted to capture them; about the demeanor and somewhat hostile behavior of the French in the port; with serio-comic emphasis, they warned us both about the pitfalls of British filmmaking—as though either of us might be about to launch ourselves into it—and such a myriad of subjects that although I stood there motionless and listening ravenously, I felt I was tumbling down a mountainside, an avalanche a few yards behind me.

Unlike her brother Fermin, my mother had not a trace of a foreign accent, although as I learned over the next few months, she spoke English with a foreigner's extreme caution, as though entering an unexplored forest full of dangers. She wanted, I guessed, to speak impeccably, and she would often pause in the middle of a sentence to make a kind of grammar drama. "Is it sort or kind?" "Is it were or was?" "Is it me or I?" she would ask, pondering the perilous choices and looking up at the ceiling as though it might contain the answer.

Now, in mid-sentence, she switched to Spanish and bent suddenly to embrace my grandmother with nearly human warmth as if she'd all at once recalled that the elderly woman standing so submissively behind her, a stunned smile on her face, was her own mother, who, with her poor grasp of

English, would not have understood even a part of what had been said.

My mother's eyes stared at me over my grandmother's shoulder. Her mouth formed a cold radiant smile. My soul shivered.

My father leaned toward me at that moment, reaching out a hand to push a clump of hair behind my ear. The tips of his fingers were damp. He laughed. He murmured, "Well, pal. Well, well. . . . Here we all are."

I had been told by some relative that my father wrote for the movies. During the month that followed their return from Europe, he sold a script to a Hollywood studio for $10,000, a sum beyond my comprehension. It was titled *The Last Train from Madrid.* When I visited my mother, decades later, a few months before she died, she reported to me with a roguish smile that Graham Greene had said it was "the worst movie I ever saw." She chuckled—if a Spaniard can ever be said to chuckle.

After two days, they left the small Manhattan hotel that they had gone to directly from the ship and took a room at the Half-Moon Hotel on the boardwalk at Coney Island, a ramshackle pile at the best of times that burned down long ago.

My father said they were too "broke" to afford the first hotel. Something about his tone of voice suggested to me that being "broke" was a temporary condition and that it was different from being poor.

He told me he'd written the entire movie in a week while Elsie, my mother, handed him Benzedrine tablets from the bed upon which she lay, doing crossword puzzles and lighting cigarette after cigarette.

My grandmother and I visited them there one afternoon. During the hour or so we spent with them, my father presented me with a typewriter, a Hermès baby featherweight, saying, "Don't hock it, I may want it back." Only a few days later, he did just that, taking it back with a muttered explanation I couldn't quite make out.

During that same visit, he said he had heard about a bequest of $50 made me by "La Señora Ponvert" of Olmiguero. I didn't look at my grandmother. Who else could have told him? He asked to borrow it, swearing he would repay me—spoken as though we both, he and I, understood that money was nothing; and the old lady leaving it to me, and the amount itself, were trivial matters compared to the larger reality of existence itself; and at this vertiginous moment, my mother spoke from the chair where she was sitting, looking through the pages of a newspaper.

"Tía Luisa," she said, without glancing up at me. I had forgotten, not that it was the same person they both had mentioned, but that there had been a bequest. I looked at my grandmother, who was nodding her head rapidly and saying, Yes, yes, in a nearly inaudible voice as though she had been considering that very matter and had arrived at the fortunate conclusion that she and I would make the journey downtown in New York City to the bank where the money was and withdraw it at once.

When my father sold the movie in a week or so—it was easier in those days, simpler—he didn't offer either to pay back the fifty dollars or to return the typewriter. And I, feeling that both "loans" would be judged by my parents as trivial, never mentioned them. I hadn't cared about the money, but I had liked the typewriter.

Once my father had been paid for the movie, he bought his own father an enormous radio that he had delivered to the house in Yonkers on Warburton Avenue. And he arranged for me to meet Elsie at De Pinna's department store on Fifth Avenue who would buy me some clothes.

There was little danger in the subways and the streets in those days. A child was safer, except for the occasional flasher lurking at the dark end of a station platform who might emerge like the spirit of an abandoned cave, exposing his genitals with a glazed look on his face. Yet as I rode into the city from Kew Gardens, I felt an alarm pervading me I couldn't put a name to.

I saw Elsie before she saw me. She was moving indolently toward the glove counter close to the store entrance. She looked so isolated yet so complete in herself. It was as though someone using a brushful of black paint had blocked out all the figures walking around her.

She appeared to sense my presence, or perhaps the presence of a person staring at her intently. She turned toward me as I drew nearer. "Oh. There you are," she said formally. Her smile was meant for great things.

The shoe department was on another floor, and I guessed we were to begin there. We went to the elevator, my mother keeping a certain distance between us. From time to time, she glanced at my footwear. I felt ashamed, as though it were I who had made it unfit for her eyes.

She bought me two pairs of handsome shoes, one black kidskin, the other green suede. During the time we were together, it felt as if we were being continually introduced to each other. I was conscious of an immense strain, as though a large limp animal hung from my neck, its fur impeding my speech.

Each time, each sentence, I had to start anew. I could hear effort in her voice, too. The whole transaction, selecting, fitting, paying, wrapping, took less than twenty-five minutes. She smiled brilliantly at me in the elevator descending; the smile lasted a few seconds too long.

"Can you get home by yourself?" she asked me, as though I had suddenly strayed into the path of her vision. I nodded wordlessly. The shopping was over.

I watched her walk away up Fifth Avenue with her peculiar stride, so characteristic that in the few weeks she'd been back in the United States, I'd learned to imitate it. Half the time she would tiptoe as though she were ready to fly off the earth.

For years afterward, I thought about that stride of hers, and now and then, when I was alone, I found myself using it as I crossed the floor of the apartment. It was an expression of her strangeness, her singularity—even, if remotely, of her glamour.

I tried wearing the green suede shoes with Natalie's green flowered dress, which, as I'd grown taller, fitted me better. But the combination didn't work. And I had no other clothes to match the elegance of the shoes. They gathered dust in my grandmother's closet. When I left for good, I left the shoes there too.

My grandmother, given energy and hope by a slight increase in her monthly check from the Ponvert estate—and perhaps by the return of her daughter, perhaps not—found in the same building a larger apartment with a separate bedroom.

We moved into it along with Uncle Vincent, who appeared at the front door carrying a small suitcase just as we finished putting things away.

He slept on the studio couch in the living room and, after a few months, departed with no more explanation than he had given upon his arrival.

He went elsewhere to practice the piano which, I learned years later, he had taught himself to play. He had a telephone installed, so he could be reached for playing engagements to accompany violinists or singers on their way up or down the concert ladder. After he left, it rang only when one or the other of my parents called.

Vincent had violent nightmares. His screams of terror woke me, piercing my dreams. In the throes of one, he kicked a hole in the thin plaster of the wall just above the couch. The next morning, my grandmother taped over the hole a photograph she had cut from an issue of *Life* magazine of a melancholy ape sitting on a tree stump in the middle of a shallow lake.

She had saved it to show to Leopold, who had been living on the East Side of Manhattan in an apartment ever since the Audley Street house was sold. She always strove to please him, to evoke his laughter. He took an ironic pleasure in all forms of life, especially the simian ones.

Some Sundays the three unmarried sons, Leopold, Vincent, and Frank, came to have lunch with their mother at a table in the dinette. It was a tight space for even the two of us.

When my grandmother or I cleared the table, Leopold, warily and wearily, would start a conversation with Vincent, who might suddenly interrupt him with a comment unrelated to the subject. Tension would grow, especially if Frank was away.

My stomach trouble, diagnosed by the Cuban doctor, would flare up on those Sundays. I'd excuse myself from the table and go to the bedroom I continued to share with my grandmother, clutching my belly, trying to find a position that would give me some relief from the spasms.

When none of his brothers was present, Leopold would turn up with a young man, slim-waisted, graceful, comely, who would present my grandmother with a bouquet of flowers that smelled strongly of subway stations.

When only Vincent sat at the round table, he would speak to his mother in a pitiless voice, describing the heavy silverware he had been privileged to use "only last weekend," at other tables, provided by rich elderly women in whose company, I gathered, he spent much of his time.

His words were accompanied by grimaces, throat-clearing, low mutters of "Yes . . . yes," as though in agreement with himself.

His scornful glance would fall upon the cheap silverware his mother set beside his plate, and he held up a fork as if it were evidence of a particularly low crime.

He went soundlessly, abruptly, on errands that were as mysterious to me as they were—I presumed—irresistible to him. I imagined using his suspenders like a slingshot and catapulting him out the door, to land on the black-and-white tiles of the building's bleak hallway.

A box arrived shortly after he did, holding a few books. Prominently featured was a return address of the apartment house we lived in. He had sent them to himself, but where had he been when he mailed them?

He entered a room like Conrad Veight in the movie *The Cabinet of Dr. Caligari*, giving the impression he was creeping along a wall. Quick as a flash, he had fits of anger like the scattering light of a lamp knocked from a table, veering wildly, lasting seconds.

He laughed at a private thought; his eyes disappeared, squeezed shut; without revealing what it was, he insisted it was remarkably funny. I sensed in him a rage at all human endeavor.

One of the rich old women he knew died in her suite at the Waldorf. To my amazement, she left me, a stranger, a trunkful of clothes.

"By Worth of Paris," Vincent said, looking at something in a corner of the living room. "The name has significance in Paris. He is an eminent designer of women's clothes. Yes, yes," he said, as if Worth's triumph was his own. I flinched at his tone, but my heart was leaping like a hooked fish. I was envisioning glorious clothes.

"Your mother took the trunk and its contents." He was nearly shouting at me. "She observed that the clothes were too mature for you." He nodded rapidly and added, with a ghastly smile, "Far, far too old." Turning on his heel, he left the apartment on one of his errands.

Years later, I came to see how an implacable enmity toward Jews and all things Jewish distorted the views of two of Candelaria's children, Vincent and Elsie. Anti-Semitism made them into aging Latin skinheads.

The books Vincent had mailed to himself were repulsive tracts about the "Jewish question." My mother, after a few drinks, would begin a conversation with friends of my father's with, "You Jews—"

She claimed enchantment with another Semitic people, the Bedouin. "So romantic," she would murmur, smiling to herself.

Perhaps, I would think later, she and Vincent suspected Jewish ancestors in their own family.

A prominent rabbi came to see my grandmother. He was trying to trace a branch of his family. My grandmother welcomed him. Vincent, at home that day, told him to leave "at once."

"*El pobre,*" said my grandmother, a lapsed Catholic—although that suggests a religiosity she didn't have. She had simply drifted away from the church.

I thought her effusively "tolerant" toward Jews, and boastful about her tolerance. When I was grown, I realized she hadn't been boasting so much as trying to offset the savage bias shared by Elsie and Vincent, the only thing they had in common.

A few weeks after Vincent told me about the trunk of Worth clothes, Fermin came to see his mother. I went quickly into the bedroom.

After an hour or so, she called to me and asked me to see him to the door. We didn't say a word to each other. But upon reaching it, he suddenly turned to me and, to my horror, dropped to his knees, holding up his hands as if praying. "Forgive me!" he cried, bursting into tears.

It was a blinding moment of confusion for me. Yet I noticed

a spot of bristles on his chin he had missed while shaving with the straight razor I knew he used, and this brought to mind the black razor strop. One Sunday, in a rage, he had taken the strop off the bathroom hook and, laying about himself, managed to hit everyone within his reach. My grandmother was taking a walk with Elpidia and had left me in the flat, so I caught it too. But Natalie got the worst of it, a vicious blow across the back.

Now I was getting the worst of it in a different way: confronted by a kneeling adult, tears running across his prominent cheekbones and into his crocodile mouth.

Several months after my parents had returned from Europe, I found myself alone with them in the bedroom my grandmother and I shared. She was talking with Leopold in the living room. It was late afternoon.

My mother lay down on the bed on her side, holding her head with palm pressed against cheek. My father was lying on his back, his head on a pillow, and I was half reclining between them. They looked at me gravely as I spoke about music I had heard. I wanted to speak to them about what I imagined they loved.

It was a long moment, lasting a few minutes or an hour. I don't know which. Some sort of sympathy flowed among us. I wanted to keep it forever.

Later, I regretted I had spoken so adoringly of a tenor of that period, Nino Martini, and claimed to have heard whole operas when I knew only arias from them. Yet for years I thought about this moment with my parents, an intimacy out of time, larger than language.

In December of that year, my grandmother and I took a train to Cape Cod and then a boat to Martha's Vineyard, where my parents had rented a house in Edgartown.

We were to spend the long Christmas weekend with them. It would be their first holiday season in the United States in years. My father met our ferry. He stood on a pier, his hands in his jacket pockets, looking out at the stormy waters of the bay. He looked a heroic figure, and there was a statuelike quality about his stance that gave me the impression he knew it.

As he was stowing our luggage in the trunk of the car, I stole a glance at his jacket, the most dashing one I had ever seen. Of course I knew very little about jackets. He caught my look. It was a Norfolk jacket, he said, one he'd bought in London during the years he had lived in England and worked for a British movie studio, writing screenplays. He said it was named after the Duke of Norfolk, a hereditary peer.

I was overwhelmed by all that I didn't know, my bottomless ignorance. Words slipped from his mouth laden with meaning: silent explosions lighting up worlds that had been dark before he spoke.

In an upstairs room of the small weathered shingle house, he was writing a novel.

* * *

My mother said, neutrally, that other children in the neighborhood were able to amuse themselves; they didn't seem to need adults to be involved with their pastimes. With a disinclined air, she taught me how to play solitaire.

My father introduced me to Jimmy Cagney, who was sitting in his idling car on the main street of Edgartown. His clump of a hand, covered with reddish freckles, rested on the window rim.

A minute earlier, Daddy had said loudly, "There's Cagney!"

"Do you know him?" I asked.

"Of course not," he replied, walking ahead of me to cross the street. "Come on. Don't go all maidenly and shy, for crissakes. . . ."

Cagney was small and compact. I could see he was thinking of something else as he exchanged greetings with my father. Daddy's voice was nervy, boastful. I kept my eyes on Cagney's hand, which hadn't moved from the window. I thought I saw the skin tighten.

I heard my father say, as we walked away from the car, "He has a house on the island." He seemed apologetic, weakened, and I thought of how the notability of a man turns everyone around him into beggars.

I saw a dartboard hanging on the dining room wall. Daddy said dartboards hung in all the pubs in England and explained how the game was played. A handful of darts lay nearby. I picked up one and threw it. It landed on the tip of another that was already in the bull's-eye. Daddy, passing at that moment, said, "I'll give you a hundred bucks if you do that again."

He carefully removed the dart I had thrown. I threw another, feeling possessed by dark powers, and saw the thrown dart quivering in the end of the first.

"My God!" he shouted. "You did it!" My mother entered the room frowning. When she'd heard what he'd promised me, she exclaimed fiercely, "Puppy! You can't! You can't do that!"

But he did, holding out crumpled bills to me that I handed over to my grandmother. It was further evidence of my poor character—in my mother's eyes and in mine. I was assailed by nameless fears. I stared at the dartboard as if it might tell me what I had done.

After our return to Kew Gardens, my grandmother bought me a winter coat with part of the winnings. What she did with the rest of it, I don't know.

My mother retired to her bed, where she spent the rest of the day, a hot-water bottle on her abdomen. I heard my father's voice as he took her cups of hot water to ease the pain of the "gut trouble" she was prone to. My grandmother and I crept around the house, trying not to make noise. Elsie's misery sent out waves of repressive holiness.

Daddy and I took a long walk along an ocean beach a few miles from Edgartown. It was a winter sea, the air damp, the water the color of gunmetal. As the mild surf broke at our feet, Daddy talked. Unlike the last time when he had spoken of books, he was sober.

The interior of the country was abhorrent to him. He feared those vast stretches of prairie and mountain, those flat plains, the towns and cities populated by characters out of *Main Street*, those Babbitts—

"What are they?" I interrupted.

"Sinclair Lewis wrote novels about them," he replied, with a broad gesture of his arm that took in the whole beach and the bluffs above it.

He had wanted to be a teacher, he said. But he had sold a story to *Smart Set*. A few days later, the telephone rang in the Morning-side house he lived in then with his family. He was nineteen and dazed by the call from H. L. Mencken, the editor of the magazine. Mencken invited him to lunch at Delmonico's. He had been so overwhelmed he couldn't even glance at the menu and ordered scrambled eggs.

In the late Twenties and early Thirties, my father was writing screenplays for a Hollywood studio, along with other scriptwriters. He was drinking a good deal. So was F. Scott Fitzgerald, whom he knew. "A minor poet," he said dismissively.

One of the people he was close to was Vincent Lawrence, the man who had met my train from Redlands and taken me to the miniature golf course. Another was an English playwright, Benn Levy, temporarily a screenwriter too. Benn

Levy had put him in a car when he had passed out from liquor, driven him to the Mojave desert and a shack he had rented in advance, and left him there with a typewriter, a cot, groceries for a week, and a table. Benn had had the foresight to hire an ex-sailor, a grizzled elderly man, to bring him a barrel of fresh water once a week. After my father sobered up, cursing Benn for a couple of days, he began to write his first novel, *Sailor Town*.

"Were there snakes?" I asked.

"Yes. One morning I discovered an enormous rattlesnake curled in a corner," he answered. I gasped.

He had run to his cot, he told me. The snake wriggled out of the shack while Daddy stared at it over the edge of a thin blanket he'd covered himself with.

"Snakes can bite through thin blankets," I said, consulting my imagination.

"I know," Daddy replied.

I didn't believe him, but I didn't think he was lying. Or rather, I believed in the power of stories. Perhaps he didn't tell them all to me that day on the beach. Perhaps the stories were told over several days and evenings of that visit, and in later meetings with my father. They struck me as a way of thinking, of finding out the weakness of given attitudes and so-called truths inherited by the generations. There was no final truth.

There were two English brothers, the Stokers, and they bet on the question of who could write the most frightening story.

Bram Stoker won when he wrote *Dracula*. Until then, he had written books for children.

There was a South American ant that carried a leaf over its head; there were other ants, called army ants, that could destroy a plantation house.

The French Revolution had begun because cooks in aristocratic households made *cotelettes à la victime*; three lamb chops on a skewer held over a fire. The cooks threw away the top and bottom chops for the benefit of the remaining one.

He'd been a play fixer as well as a playwright. Play fixing was emergency help for ailing plays. One had opened in Boston, Louis Calhern in the lead role. When Calhern saw that the audience consisted of five people, he stepped forward and invited them on stage to join the cast.

Among our ancestors was Lord Fairfax of Virginia, who had given a young surveyor employment. The young surveyor was George Washington.

He had been "thrown out" of five colleges because "rules were made to be broken."

I listened desperately, time-haunted, rapt. Now and then I asked a question. Daddy would preface his answer with the assertion, "I hear what you're saying beneath that!" It gratified me with its implication that there was a deeper meaning to my words than even I understood. If only I could discover what I really meant! I worked like a mole, tunneling always deeper for meaning, attributing nuance where there was none.

When it was too windy for the beach, we walked through the streets of Edgartown. He knew people everywhere, I thought to myself, as we went into a real estate agent's office, where a black stove sent out the fragrance of woodsmoke. I began to feel nostalgic for a past that wasn't mine.

During that visit, on a late afternoon, I heard him singing "Smiles" to himself. His voice was light and filled with a kind of random tenderness. But his mood changed when he began to amuse himself by replacing "All who love are blind" in the song "Smoke Gets in Your Eyes" with "You and who else besides . . . ?" He prolonged "besides" until his voice gave out.

When my grandmother and I boarded the ferry in Vineyard Haven to leave the island, my parents stood on the pier. As the boat made its ungainly turn, my mother walked away, but my father stayed until he was a shadow on the horizon.

I was wretched at the idea of returning to Kew Gardens. But I didn't dare contemplate a change in my life. The stars, after all, were fixed in the heavens.

I read a novel, *The Last Days of Pompeii.* It was thrilling to know that the city had been preserved at the moment of its destruction in A.D. 79, even as people went about their daily lives. I found photographs of its villas, its chariot-grooved cobblestone streets. Like a fly in amber, it was a manuscript of life as it had been, to be read again and again, readings accompanied by incredulity at the literalness of preserved objects: loaves of bread, artisans' shops, dog on a chain, bodies.

My parents borrowed an apartment on the top floor of an East Side brownstone in New York City. A flight of dimly lit carpeted stairs led to their rooms. I made a visit there. On the way up, I saw what I took to be dark bundles of laundry. When I came close to one, I realized it was a huddled silent child, staring at me through the balusters. There was something queer about her face. Her round head was covered with straight straw-colored hair. I said hello. She smiled at once, as if until I had actually spoken she didn't know what kind of creature I was.

Other bundles stood ahead of me, crouching or standing up and leaning on the stair railing. I learned they were brain-damaged children in the care of the German doctor who owned the house. I heard more about him subsequently than I wanted to hear.

I came to know the title of his favorite song, "Wien," that he drank heavily, and that his practice was limited to those children. My mother had had an affair with him, she told me a few years later. She made no effort to soften, justify, or explain the affair, the same way she told me she had once "gone to bed" with a South American relative for a mink coat he had promised her. "We've always, Paul and I, been so broke," she said, in a detached tone of voice.

When the German doctor died, she went to his grave and poured a pint of whiskey on the earth above his coffin.

During that visit to my parents, my father told me he intended to take me to Europe, then to the island of Capri. A fisherman could be hired there to row one to a marvelous grotto. My heart jumped. I asked if we could sail over on the *Queen Elizabeth*.

Daddy scowled. "What a dreadful little materialist you are!" he exclaimed. I didn't know what a materialist was, but I knew it was odious to him. In Elsie's presence, I had noticed, he tended to get angry with me.

My mother said, "It's a natural thing to want at her age," and smiled at me. I was astonished that she had defended me. It was the first time.

Elsie, too, had stories and sayings. One of the former took place in Tijuana, a Mexican border town. She and my father had gone there for a weekend. They registered in the only hotel, then went to the long bar, a well-known place to tourists.

He drank himself into a stupor. She left for the hotel. Hours later, he stumbled into their room. She telephoned the desk clerk and, in Spanish, told him there was a drunken stranger in her room. Mexican police came to arrest him and take him off to "the pokey," she told me, with the condescension some foreigners exhibit when they use American slang.

He spent the night in jail and didn't speak to her for hours when he was released the next morning into her custody. She was wildly amused by the episode.

She had an idea for a ballet she told me about several times. There would be dancers costumed as houseflies.

Love and death, struggle and triumph, and suddenly immense shoes appear on stage and advance. They hold the feet of a monstrous charwoman whom the audience never sees, only her broom, sweeping the flies and their dramas away.

After reading a news story about farmers shooting coyotes, she said, "Why not arm the coyotes?

"What if it's *cancer* that catches *people*?" she asked. "Cancer says, Look out! Here comes a human!" And how tiresome it was to hear someone speak of the stars and how small they and the universe made him feel. "What huge egotism to feel so small when it's all relative," she said. Each story, each saying, illustrated an aspect of her nature. I didn't know how to put them together for a long time.

Florida

I did not regret saying goodbye to my grandmother. I was going with my parents to Florida, to a house owned, and infrequently used, by a friend of my mother's. It was an hour or so south of Jacksonville. I would be where I wanted to be at last, I supposed.

I stared at my mother, who drove holding a cigarette in one hand. Smoke and her dark hair blew toward me in the small backseat of the roadster. The top was down. The car had been bought, my father said, with movie money.

My heart was hardened toward my grandmother. I blamed her for taking me from Uncle Elwood. There were days when I forgave her nothing. Then even her walk irritated me. She had foot trouble, bunions and corns. I disliked the way she tottered about. She often said, "I know many t'ings," and I greeted my father's imitation of her words with more merriment than I felt, as though she could see and hear me laughing at her.

Once, she had kept me from visiting a friend in the evening. She clutched her breast as I went to the door, crying weakly, "*¡Ay, mi corazón!*" as though she were having a heart attack. I reluctantly gave in, though I was unable to believe her expression of suffering genuine. The idea that she *was* suffering, because of her anxiousness about what might happen to me, never crossed my mind.

Sometimes she tried to amuse me with stories; I was cold and refused to smile. Some days I would forget my resentment, released from the sullen sour feeling that troubled my own heart, until animosity toward her would overcome me again.

My parents took turns driving, she expertly, he clumsily. We stopped at a diner, where I ate, uneasily, two fried egg sandwiches. Elsie watched me, forming, I was sure, conclusions about my character.

South of East Jacksonville, we turned off the highway onto a sand road. It ended in a heavily wooded area where there was a scattering of homes on the banks of the broad St. John's River. Close to a bluff stood a large, shambling, yellow-painted house inhabited by an elderly Scottish woman named Lesser, the house-keeper. She maintained an expression of bland benevolence on her face throughout the confusion of the weeks that followed, and I began to attribute it entirely to the physical configuration of her features.

The high-ceilinged rooms were large and barely furnished.

Below the bluff a gray wharf on crooked posts stood in the river. Everywhere I looked were floating patches of hyacinths in whose tangled roots—I learned later—water moccasins liked to shelter.

First times were events: the first time I had been on a car trip with my parents, the first time we'd been in a diner, the first time we had eaten supper together in the dining room of the yellow house, served by Mrs. Lesser.

My mother's silence emphasized my father's volubility. Nervousness pitched his voice higher than ever before. One night I spoke hesitantly of George Bernard Shaw, one of whose plays I had read recently to please my father. My mother rose abruptly from the table, overturning her chair, and ran up the stairs. Daddy followed her into the bathroom. I could hear them quarreling, and I noticed my father's voice was pleasing even when he was angry. I stayed at the foot of the stairs, not knowing what to do.

My father appeared in the upper hall and behind him stood Elsie. She called my name. Holding a napkin carelessly in his hand, he came down and walked into the dining room, shrugging his shoulders and murmuring, "I don't know, pal, what she's up to."

I went up the stairs, and my mother turned to go into the bathroom, where she sat on the rim of the tub. A fleeting impression of her inability to assume an ungraceful posture sped through my mind, along with my dread of what she would say.

"You have no right to speak to Paul about George Bernard Shaw," she said, without raising her head. "You have no right to tie your father's shoelaces."

My hopes for I don't know what withered. I was appalled by her assumption that I had been insolent—at least that's what I thought it was that had evoked such words from her. She pushed herself upright and quelled me with a look before she walked into their bedroom.

Two or three days later, they left Florida to return to New York City. During that time, my mother was polite to me. When I looked at her, she smiled neutrally.

As they drove off, I felt they had not left me so much as forgotten my existence. I was trapped by my age, twelve. I was obligated to stay on with Mrs. Lesser.

I walked into the kitchen as soon as they had driven away. The housekeeper looked up at me from shelling peas on the counter. Her neat hair, the cleanness of her apron, and her expression all conveyed to me that she attributed disorder to moral failing, whether it was in a dusty closet or in people's lives.

Disorder was defeat.

She kept her own counsel, she was discreet, but she rebelled secretly with her whole being against the agitation she had sensed during their stay of a few days. It was undignified to allow oneself to be baffled, though she would forgive it in children.

She took a few steps toward me and said, with a trace of a

kindly smile, "We'll have to find a nearby school for you next month." It was during a day in August.

I went to a public school in East Jacksonville. Every weekday morning a school bus picked me up, and in the afternoon it dropped me off at the edge of the woods.

Spanish moss hung from tree branches and brushed against my face like thick cobwebs. One afternoon, a snake dropped from a limb onto my shoulders before it slid to the ground and twisted away. It happened so quickly, I didn't have time for horror. Horror struck me a few minutes later when I reached the house. I must have been pale enough to attract Mrs. Lesser's attention. She asked me what was wrong and I told her. "God preserve us!" she said.

The teacher of the seventh-grade civics class was a short man with a clever face. I sat in the last row with Lee, a tall, thin, handsome boy. Our civics textbooks were opened to conceal a travel book by Osa and Martin Johnson. We were reading it with romantic intensity, thinking of each other's appreciation. Suddenly we sensed the teacher's presence as we turned a page.

"Interesting," he murmured. "But out of place, don't you think?"

Matt, a melancholy boy of ten who lived in a shabby plantation house a few hundred yards from the yellow house, took me out on the river in his small motorboat to catch the swells from the big ships that sailed in and out of Jacksonville.

He advised me to jump on the wharf two or three times before venturing out on it. The thumping chased away the moccasins, which fell one by one from the wharf posts where they had been coiled and hidden, dropping into the water like thick gray ropes.

One afternoon after school, we went up a narrow stream that emptied into the big river. We ducked to avoid low branches that arched over the water. Snakes could fall on us at any moment, but we were fearless, at least for those minutes when we pretended we were sailing up the Congo.

The Scottish housekeeper employed a small black girl to do the chores she couldn't manage because of severe arthritis in her hands. Mattie, like Matt, was ten.

One afternoon I followed her flickering shadow through the woods a minute after Mrs. Lesser told her she could go home. She led me to a clearing where a little church with two tiny windows, looking like a child's drawing, stood as if held upright. I found a wooden crate and dragged it to one of the windows and stepped up on it.

Mattie was standing in a roughly nailed pulpit, her thin body concealed by a white robe that billowed as she swayed. She was "testifying," as she told me later. She was a burning coal of spirit in the church, itself as makeshift as the wooden crate.

We often played in the fenced-in yard behind the yellow house. Mattie's eyes would suddenly focus on something I couldn't see. Turning around, I'd find the housekeeper in the kitchen doorway, her soft plump hand holding the screen door open for Mattie to come back into the kitchen, where she might have to lift something, or stir a thickening pudding, or run through the woods to the plantation house to borrow a sweet pepper from Matt's mother.

When I arrived home one afternoon, Mattie walked toward me holding an object in her hand, a small peach-colored leather pocketbook, worn and scratched as though it had been worried by a Florida lynx, with a loose metal clasp in the form of an X. She handed it to me shyly, watching my face. Just as shyly I took it, not sure whether she was giving it or showing it to me. Was it hers? Had she found it on a road where it might have been tossed through a car window by an angry woman? No. She was making a present of it to me.

Lee drove me to his house half an hour distant. The day was brilliant, still. Not a leaf stirred. The narrow country road had a blue cast, and the mica in the paving was struck into sparks by the sunlight. He stopped the car.

A huge snake was stretched across the road, its middle swollen. He got out of the car, looked thoughtfully at the snake, and then bent to gather it up like wet washing and carry it to a ditch on the side of the road.

Lee had an earnest, grave quality, perhaps because he was a scientific boy. After introducing me to his mother, he took me upstairs to his room at the front of the house. The windows overlooked a branch of the river. A microscope stood on a broad table covered with plant cuttings. It was beautiful there, the big house off by itself, a research laboratory in a wilderness of trees and water. I looked at a bug and a leaf through the microscope lens.

On my thirteeth birthday, he drove to the yellow house in his Ford flivver with a gift, a very tall white lily in a small red pot.

My other friend was a girl named Marjorie. Her life was a perpetual melodrama. She would greet me with the words—or a variation of them—"Guess what's happened to me now!"

That spring three people came for a few days: my father, my Spanish grandmother, and the owner of the yellow house.

Daddy arrived on a rainy afternoon, driving the car in which he and my mother had brought me to Florida in August. He had been shaken up on the way by nearly running into a dead cow lying on the road. It suddenly loomed out of the darkness in the headlights. His first day, the cow continued to loom before him in the shadows. He kept muttering "Jesus!" I could see by his face how it had shocked him, was still shocking him.

He took me with him to a bench on the bluff from which we looked down at the wharf and the river. He had something to tell me, the reason he had driven a thousand miles.

He and Elsie were getting a divorce.

I had not thought of them as married. How could it be that

Elsie was enough of an organic being to have carried me in her belly for a term? What I was sure of was that fate had determined that her presence was the price I had to pay in order to see my father. But when I did see him, his behavior with me—playful, sometimes cruel, a voice of utterly inconsistent and capricious authority—confirmed my uneasiness, my ever-growing sense of being an imposter, outside life's laws.

But he had more to tell me. The second piece of news, preceded by the word "tragic," was that Uncle Leopold was a homosexual. I was uncertain of what that meant. What I found nearly unbearable was the idea that Leopold should now know that I knew. Daddy said it was a crucial deviation from custom. Leopold couldn't help it, he said. What was it he couldn't help?

I owned a secret full of danger, one that would so humiliate Leopold if I revealed it that he would cease to care for me.

My father suddenly changed the subject. "Here! I don't want you smoking behind my back!" he said, and held out a crumpled pack of Camel cigarettes. I shook my head no, still thinking about Leopold. Soon we were wrestling, only half humorously. The outcome was that I found a lit cigarette in my mouth.

I didn't take to smoking right away, but a few weeks later Marjorie and I lit up, coughed, and persisted.

Nothing more was said about Leopold, divorce, or cigarettes during the three days he spent in the yellow house.

The housekeeper asked him to cut down a dead tree that stood in the yard. I watched him use the ax. His face was taut with concentration as he deepened the cleft in the trunk. I put my hand to my throat. When the tree toppled, it made a noise between a groan and a shriek and appeared to me to fall in slow motion, a tree in a myth.

On the last morning, after he said goodbye to Mrs. Lesser, whom he had charmed with his half-serious attentions, I walked with him to the car. I told him I hoped someone, by now, had removed the dead cow from the road. "Dear pal," he said, pressing my shoulder with his hand.

I watched him drive away down the sand road until the car vanished among the trees. He had taught me the rudiments of driving during his first visit with Elsie. He was a good teacher, explaining everything clearly and without impatience. I noticed, before the car disappeared, how he gripped the steering wheel and reared up in a spasm of panic, as if he expected at any moment for the car to run amok.

The second visit was from the owner of the house and Mrs. Lesser's employer. Her name was Mary. She arrived with a friend, Thweeny. A few years earlier, they had both graduated from Smith College, along with the housekeeper's daughter.

Mary had fair curling hair, and, in the mornings of the week they stayed, she wore a pale pink linen housecoat to breakfast that I admired. She was pretty, with blue eyes that resembled my father's. She had brought me a present, a book of Katherine Mansfield's short stories, *The Pear Tree*. She paid attention to me and behaved as if we were the same age.

Thweeny was a tall bony woman, a large rag doll whose limbs flew around like windmill sails. Her long dark hair hung down to her shoulders in strips like licorice. She was clownish and likable.

Mary told me Thweeny had been raped when she was thirteen. I knew in a general way what rape was. After I had heard about it, I looked at her with more interest.

One morning the three of us got into the car and drove to St. Augustine. Mary brought along her camera. Except for Uncle Elwood, she was the only adult who took pictures of me.

I told her my father was getting a divorce. I said I hoped she would marry him. She said she was my mother's friend.

Mary and Thweeny left, and my grandmother arrived to spend a few days in the yellow house. I often interrupted a huddle in the kitchen between the two women. Once I heard the housekeeper exclaim, "Shocking!" I didn't know what they were gossiping about. I found my grandmother's presence oppressive. Her long looks at me and her sighs had a damp physical weight. She paid no attention to the house or the woods or the river. Her landscape was interior, the countryside of her emotions.

My father unexpectedly appeared again, to drive me back to New York. Before we left we made a visit to the bench on the bluff. From a house on our right, partly hidden by tropical foliage, a familiar-looking woman emerged. I had forgotten her name, but she greeted me as she walked past us on the narrow path.

She had glanced disapprovingly at my father. Later that same day, she came to the back door of the house and asked the house-keeper for me. When I came to the door, she whispered that my mother was telephoning from New York City and wanted to speak with me.

In those days a long-distance call was uncommon and usually meant an emergency. I followed the neighbor to her house. The telephone receiver was lying beside the base. I picked it up and listened. I heard breathing. Elsie said, "Is that you, Paula?" I said yes. She then asked, as if she already knew the answer, "Do you love me?"

Who was I to love such a person, and who was she to be loved? I was frightened by her question; there was something in her voice that made loving her a punishment. But I said yes. I was painfully aware of the neighbor listening nearby.

She asked me to get hold of Mary's diary and read it to her. She gave me the telephone number of where she would be waiting for my call. "But Mary's not here," I protested weakly. Elsie answered that she would arrive any day now. She explained what a diary was, as though I were brain damaged. I agreed to do what she asked, though I didn't mean to, any more than I intended to return her call.

Mary arrived the very next day. I was so tormented by the turmoil I felt, by the neighbor's evident dislike of my father, by the news about Leopold he had given me, by Elsie's telephone call, that when Daddy asked me sternly what was troubling me, I burst into sobs.

The two of us were sitting on the bench. It suddenly occurred to me I could run away. But to what? My parents filled the world.

Daddy put his arm around my waist. "There, there," he murmured.

"Elsie telephoned me and asked me to read her Mary's diary," I said, immensely relieved to tell him.

He only said, "Things will be better soon." We sat there for a long while.

Mattie and Matt came to say goodbye. Lee brought me a twenty-page letter to read on the way north. Marjorie cried, as she often did, about things both large and small. I saw a tear run down Matt's soft, freckled cheek. Mattie smiled and held my hand for a minute.

As the three of us drove away, Mary, Daddy, and I, with the housekeeper waving her apron goodbye, goodbye, I was struck by the thought that the last weeks had resembled a Marx Brothers movie: people rushing in and out of the yellow house, drawing themselves up, making peculiar faces, attacking, retreating.

Somehow, I had managed to get through classes. I had one more year until high school.

I returned to my grandmother's apartment in Kew Gardens, leaving my father and Mary in her Greenwich Village apartment. I went back to P.S. 99 and, following Mary's example, began to keep a diary. I had written in it every day for only a few weeks—the entries were self-conscious and stiff—when I discovered my grandmother reading it behind the bedroom door.

She was flustered and her face turned red. She said she had picked it up from a table because it was so evidently new. I stared at her, hard-eyed. Then I took the diary from her unresisting hands. I wouldn't admit to myself that my intention to keep a journal had been weak from the beginning, and I had been about to stop writing in it anyway.

My grandmother told me about her father, Señor Vicente de Carvajal, and her husband, Fermin de Sola. Carvajal had come to Cuba to visit his two daughters, my grandmother and her older sister, Laura. He was said to be the best chess player in Spain, and while he was in Havana he taught a Cuban boy, known as Capablanca when he grew up, to play chess.

His daughter Laura had been sent to medical school on the island by her father. I recall a photograph of her with other members of her graduating class. Hers is a small face among bearded men. It was toward the end of the nineteenth century, and she was permitted only to enter into pediatric practice.

During my many months in Cuba, my grandmother had taken me to visit Tía Laura, my real great-aunt. She was retired, by then, and living in the country. We had supper with her and afterward went into the wild moonlit garden. A fire burned beneath a large black cauldron. I recall that she wore a black dress, silvered by the moonlight, and stirred *dulce de leche,* a Cuban sweet, with a huge ladle.

My grandmother described the row of wooden stocks she had seen on a walk with my grandfather in Cienegita. She asked him what they were for, and he replied that they were formerly used to punish slaves. Unlike the neighboring plantation owners, he abhorred slavery and had no slaves. He died in the last days of the Spanish-American War, she implied of a broken heart. When she first arrived in the United States, she had settled in Freehold, New Jersey, partly because a banker who had had business ties to her husband lived there.

She had been left with little money, some valuable jewelry, and what was left of the land, which was useless after the war, more or less permanently occupied by carpetbaggers.

One day, before going on an errand in Freehold, she took all her jewelry from the box where it was kept and spread it out on her dining table, intending to sort it. One of the children called her, and she left it lying there.

She went from child to errand, and when she returned,

the dining room window was broken and the jewelry gone.

She treated her children with the same carelessness. She went away on unexplained trips, leaving them in the charge of her eldest son, Fermin, already cruel at fifteen. He once ground out a cigarette on the back of Elsie's hand. He bullied Leopold for years. Finally, when Leopold was twelve, he turned on Fermin, chasing him up and down the streets of Freehold, brandishing a long kitchen knife whenever Fermin looked back. How I would have liked to have seen that!

When she was nearing adolescence, Elsie awoke one morning to find blood on her bedclothes. Her mother had told her nothing about menstruation. She thought she was dying. Terrified, she went to her mother. Candelaria put on her coat at once, saying she would speak with her later; the bleeding was nothing; she was due at the bank or the doctor's office, or an emergency required her to buy cough medicine for one of the boys. She went out the door of whatever place they were living in at the time.

So I envisioned the scene after Elsie told me about it, with her habitual tone of unsparing irony that diminished the meaning of everything.

When her mother left the house that morning, Elsie returned to her room, yanking at her long black hair in despair, "like someone in a mad scene from an opera," she told me. Then she stood in front of a mirror, still pulling at her hair. She wanted to watch herself, to see how tragic she appeared—so she reported, with strained gaiety.

I too found blood on the sheet when I awoke one morning, but I kept it to myself. I had learned a few things from girls in school. I asked my grandmother for money to buy what I required at the drugstore, referring to movie magazines. She must have known, somehow, what I was going to buy. She handed me the money without questioning me as she customarily did.

Across the street from school was a Dutch Reformed Church, which I joined during a brief reawakening of formal religious feeling. The church once held a lottery, toward which I gave a dollar. Elsie, visiting her mother one day and hearing from her about my contribution, asked me if I thought my dollar would make a difference in the world. I did, and I said yes. She gave me a derisive look.

I left the church a few months later, when I discovered chewing gum stuck between the pages of the hymnbook I used, and I saw a fellow choir member, a boy, grinning with a trickster's glee.

I knew both my parents were seeing other people. Perhaps in an effort to justify his interest in Mary, Daddy told me Elsie was "gone" on an editor in a New York publishing company. Still, he and she went together to New Mexico to write a movie script they hoped to sell because they were "broke." The trip was a bust. Going to New Mexico had been a dramatic gesture. They quarreled continually. After a few days, they returned to New York City, where they went their separate ways.

Soon after he came back, I met my father in a bar in the city. An editor, Maxwell Perkins, was with him to talk about a novel Daddy had written.

As he drank, my father became ever more ingratiating and expansive, gesturing and speaking oratorically. The bar was empty except for the three of us. Mr. Perkins and I were talking softly beneath my father's roaring. He asked me questions in an avuncular voice, and I answered. I had brought a small suitcase. Daddy was driving me to Pennsylvania, I informed Mr. Perkins. He said, as my father fell abruptly silent, that he hoped I would find it pleasant there.

I stayed with some of Mary's relatives in West Pittston. They lived in a large house on the banks of the Susquehanna River next to a cemetery.

Baby, Mary's cousin, was a large middle-aged woman with an abstracted, kindly face. Her hair was streaked with gray, most of it gathered in a bun at the nape of her neck, but with a few strands always drifting loosely over her features. Her husband, Henry, was tall and gaunt, heavily wrinkled, with a patch of brown hair that rested on the top of his head like a bird's nest.

Their son, David, was home from college. He had a sly, wary look. Once he tried to kiss me. His saliva was rather sour and left a part of my cheek and lower lip wet. It must have been summer; I went to bed on a sleeping porch. One morning David drove me to a Princeton track meet. His father was an alumnus. I saw Jesse Owens, a black man, win the main race.

After we returned to West Pittston, I wandered into the yard and sat down on a swing. David followed me and pushed the swing. I felt a sudden, searing pain in my belly, then another. Henry drove me to a local hospital, where a doctor examined me and diagnosed acute appendicitis.

Two or three days after the operation, Daddy came to visit me. The moment he walked into the hospital room, I began to laugh. A nurse crawled under my cot and pushed up the mattress to help me stop. I only laughed harder, clutching my incision. Daddy left.

He came back in a few minutes, and I was again seized by laughter. By his third entrance, I wept and laughed at the same time. He muttered, "For God's sake," and I was undone.

When he returned the following day, I greeted him soberly with only an occasional ripple of laughter. Each time he heard it, he raised his eyes to the ceiling in mock solemnity.

Mary brought me an edition of *The Brothers Karamazov*. I can still see an onion-domed church through the hospital window, replicated on the book's cover.

After I'd recovered from the operation, Mary paid for a few piano lessons in Pittston given to me by a tiny old man, heavily mustachioed, a former student of Leopold Godowski, a noted musician of an earlier time.

In his small studio in the boardinghouse where he lived, I

played scales and studies for beginners at his upright piano and listened to his exasperated criticism, made in a voice that crackled with irritability. He showed me a photograph of one of his other students, a young girl with long black hair, whom he praised extravagantly. "She is the one," he said, smiling at the picture.

But after my last lesson, he gave me a powerful hug. I heard and felt his tiny bones clicking beneath his musty-smelling blue suit as his mustache brushed my cheek.

The summer passed. In the first few days of September, I don't remember what day, Mary drove her friend Thweeny and me from West Pittston to New Hampshire.

Mary liked night driving. The dashboard lights lit their faces from below, and they were speaking animatedly to each other in soft voices. I was in the backseat and couldn't catch most of what they were talking about.

Mary had rented a house in Peterborough—my father was to join her later. Meanwhile, Thweeny was to stay with us. I could feel my childhood slipping away as we crossed the Berkshire Mountains. I listened to the Smith girls laugh and talk together. I was fourteen.

New Hampshire

Peterborough, New Hampshire, was a pretty New England village, comfortably ordinary, but given a certain glamour by a summer estate that had been owned by Edward Alexander MacDowell, the American composer. His widow, Marian, fulfilled his wish after his death and turned it into an artists' colony. A noted visitor had been Thornton Wilder, whose novel, *The Bridge of San Luis Rey*, I had read a year earlier. I wanted to see where he had lived and worked.

The estate was in the woods half a mile or so north of the high school I attended and, in winter, could be reached on snowshoes. My father had given me a pair for Christmas. I trudged through the hushed woods, silent save for the whisper of the snowshoes.

When I came upon fieldstone buildings, I forgot my purpose and felt only apprehension. I breathed in the gelid air. It was still except for the soft slide of snow now and then from tree branches to the ground. I peered through a mullioned window into a room already dark in the early fading of daylight.

As I strained to see deeper into the room, a vision slid into my mind of a narrow rope bridge across a deep ravine in a far-off country. All those people, the villagers of San Luis Rey, falling through the air to their deaths, conscious as they flailed their limbs when the bridge, and time itself, gave way.

The house Mary had rented in Peterborough was a replica of an Italian villa. It stood on the bank of a wide stream. Most of the windows overlooked the tumbling water. A formal garden, parklike, was on another level below the house. The stream became a waterfall there and could be glimpsed behind a line of poplars. There were iron-work benches to sit on and gravel-covered paths.

The interior of the house was a continuing surprise. The front door led directly into the living room from the street. The floors were laid with terra-cotta tiles, and the walls were surfaced with rough white plaster, both of which imparted a spare, calm loveliness to all the rooms. At the end of the living room was a large cathedral window. A corridor led to bedrooms with their own balconies overlooking the stream. One bedroom was mine.

For the first time in my life, I spent more than a few days with my father. It was what I thought normalcy to be. Mary had told the owner of the house that she was Daddy's cousin. They could have belonged to the same family, the resemblance between them was so strong; both had blue eyes and fair curly hair.

I was happy for a while. Sometimes I paused on a road that climbed a steep hill where I could look down upon the village. Standing there on winter afternoons, gripping an iron rail with a mittened hand, I watched the last violet light of the setting sun, the streetlights came on all at once like a word spoken in unison, and I felt touched by an ecstatic stillness.

An English teacher, Ilya Tracy, who wore a red silk necktie with a white shirt, cultivated my primitive love of poetry and prose. In freshman class, we memorized sections of Milton's "L'Allegro" and "Il Penseroso," Gray's "Elegy in a Country Churchyard," Shakespeare's *Julius Caesar,* and Coleridge's *Rime of the Ancient Mariner.*

One afternoon, Miss Tracy took the girls in the class on a hike. Was it in the Green or White Mountains? I forget, but I remember how, in that happy troop, I strode on pine-strewn slopes and laughed without reason along with the others.

I was on the basketball team. I had two suitors and a best friend, Beryl, who wrote poetry. One of her poems had been published in the *New Hampshire State Anthology.* My father said it was a fair imitation of Edna St. Vincent Millay. I admired that poem and her love poems about a certain senior whom I looked at curiously when we passed each other in the halls. Was he the one she embraced in a cabin by the lake where he took her in winter? Was he the one she had seen naked? Did they kiss and caress each other? Had he, as she had written, penetrated her soul and body?

I admired her so much that she managed to persuade me to give her a role I had been assigned in a play. She told me her heart would break if she wasn't on the school stage in the spring when the play was to be presented.

Carl, one of the boys interested in me, was the pharmacist's son. He left sodas in my locker that tended to tip and spill over my gym shoes. He was very short and bullet-headed, and he had a careening walk, going forward, then lurching to the side like the knight's move in chess.

The suitor I took more seriously was Jerry, a senior, a handsome Irish boy with a narrow face and crisp black curling hair. He lived north of the village in a working-class neighborhood of attached row houses. Sometimes he smelled very faintly of ketchup, perhaps because there was a ketchup factory not far from his house.

One evening he came by with two friends, Stanley and Richard. My father made a brief appearance in the living room, spoke with stately good humor, looked the boys over, and left.

They forgot me and began to talk as if I were not present, ardently, gravely. They spoke about life, about what they wanted to do in their adult lives. To be a fly on the wall was an old wish of mine. Richard had written the play with the part I had given to Beryl. Stanley wanted to be an actor. Their conversation was itself like the opening of a play.

I had a conversation with Jerry in which something besides sex held us in its grip. We were in his father's car, driving back from Keene after seeing a movie that had frightened us both. We were talking about fear.

The moon seemed to be watching us from the top of a black ridge that threw silver shadows on the road. For a moment, I wondered if my face was as guileless as his, as engrossed with what we were talking about. Love had its pretenses, its periodic withdrawals, its lies. As something to talk about, fear was safer.

I was a reed in the Christmas presentation of *The Nutcracker Suite* at the Peterborough Town Hall. Frank, a senior, known to be another senior's lover, domesticity already dawning in her eyes, ran his hands up and down my thin brown costume as I and the other reeds darted off the stage and into the wings. "Nice," he remarked, grinning.

I wondered how he could have allowed himself to have done that. I had thought him attached like a limpet to his girlfriend. I felt a tweak of triumph.

A plump dark-haired sophomore with enormous breasts was everyone's girl. She would rest up against a locker after school and all the boys could have her.

Mary came to my room some evenings. We spoke about love and sex. She wore the pink linen housecoat I was so fond of. We smoked and speculated about sexual intercourse. She was nine or ten years older than I was.

When my father and Mary were together, their topic was

usually books. An Englishman, H. W. Fowler, had written a dictionary whose definitions amused them. A series of books about the Dinsmore family might be the subject; they laughed when they spoke about the heroine's father accompanying her on her honeymoon with Mr. Trevelyan. I decided it was their form of courtship. But I didn't know whether to begin the series or not.

Daddy was working on a novel. When he was unable to write, he drank heavily, leaving the house directly after supper and returning late. Sometimes Mary drove the car down the steep hill to a bar he frequented and brought him home, protesting loudly or nearly passed out.

One night he came into my room and woke me. "I've got plans for you," he muttered. It was after midnight. His words sounded menacing. I turned on the light. His crippled stance, his bleary eyes, suggested to me that whatever held him upright was leaking away. I pitied him. He misread my expression. "Calm down, calm down. . . . I'm going to send you to a Swiss school . . . white feather beds, pure air . . . the sun striking sparks from the Alps all around you. . . . You don't believe it, do you? I'll show you!"

And he lurched away, out of the room. It took me a long time to fall asleep. I swung between belief and doubt. I'd heard these "plans" before, but I wanted to believe them.

Daddy would suddenly ask if I was having a good time, demanding that I confirm some notion of happiness he had for me. "These *are* the good old days," he would say. I had no wish to reassure him. Perhaps I wanted to get even with him for his claiming to hear what I was saying beneath what I was saying, a cause of growing division I felt in my own nature. I was becoming aware of being aware.

"One word is worth a thousand pictures," he said once, portentously. Then his tone changed into a ragging, derisive roar that made me burst into laughter.

One day I brought home a stick toy someone had given me at school. A tightrope walker balanced on a string between two pieces of wood you worked with your hands. He took it from me and imitated a witless person, looking at me with dazed booby eyes and then slowly, shakily, lowering his gaze to the toy and back to me, an imbecilic smile on his face.

He read somewhere that the actor Will Rogers had said he never met a man he didn't like. "What a horse cock!" Daddy exclaimed.

We had moved into the house in early autumn. Sometime after that, a hurricane struck. The stream that ran beside the house flooded the cellar and the garden below and blew down a giant tree at the end of the narrow street the house faced. The roots seemed to glare at me as I passed them on the way to the center of the village.

The wind raged for days. School was shut down. One night my father didn't come home at all. In the small hours, Mary drove all over Peterborough, finding him at last sleeping on a bench, his cheek on his joined hands. The bench had been carried by the floodwaters and deposited next to a bar.

The school principal had asked me to baby-sit for him during the fall. When I arrived at his house, he opened the door and welcomed me with a smile. His son was six.

In March, when he summoned me to his office, he wore a different expression. His voice grew harsher and louder as he spoke. "You people's ways are too advanced for us. It would be best if you left the school."

Years later, when I was about to matriculate at Columbia University and my transcript was needed for my brief time at Peterborough High School, I was astonished at how good my grades had been. Ilya Tracy had given me an A+.

I guessed at the reasons for the principal's asking me to leave the school. My father's drinking had escalated that spring. The local people had seen through the pretense that he and Mary were cousins.

Many years later, during a sad, desperate period of my own life that unfolded in a small town, Daddy said, "Everyone knows everything in a village the very next day."

Perhaps he had exaggerated. It took at least a week for scandal to travel. But travel it did.

New York City

My father rented a small apartment in the West Seventies from a Syrian who owned real estate all over the city. Sometimes Daddy was there, sometimes not.

I turned fifteen in the spring of 1938. Mary arranged a birthday party for me. Except for her, it was attended by men and held in an apartment owned by the same Syrian, Leopold's landlord and friend.

Mary gave me $25 to buy a dress for the occasion. I found one made of organdy that I thought as white and beautiful as a swan. But it was $33. I stood irresolutely in front of the window where the dress was displayed, uncertain of what to do. A minute later, I found myself inside the shop, speaking with an English accent to a clerk. I had no idea how preposterous I sounded.

Something besides the accent and story I told her, a story I deemed both brave and poignant, persuaded the owner to let me have the dress for $25. Her smile made me uneasy as I took the package from her hands.

On an April evening, I watched the Syrian dress in an orange ruffled rumba skirt, open to his thick waist, and a turban, decorated with fruit and flowers as fake as my English accent had been. There may have been seven or eight men, including my father and Leopold, standing around the room, talking, laughing, drinking in their various fashions, my father bolting the liquor down, holding out his glass for the Syrian to refill.

Someone sat down at the grand piano and began to play a café song, sentimental but rakish, wistful, full of chords. As he raised his face to receive the kiss of another man who leaned over him, I recognized him as my mother's lover, a German doctor who had taken care of the Down syndrome children in the brownstone house where I had gone to visit my parents.

Daddy began to ask me what I intended to do with my life. He was insistent. Wasn't I drawn to something? Wasn't there anything I wanted to make my life's work? What in hell did I want? "You have to *want* something," he said, in a hard voice.

I was frantic to answer his questions so that his reproaches would end. I began to dread his presence.

When Bernice and I had gone to Radio City years earlier, we had both averted our eyes from a sculpture in the lobby, *Spirit of the Dance*. But I had peeked and seen a larger-than-life figure of a naked kneeling woman. William Zorach was the sculptor.

"Art school," I said, when his voice was particularly merciless.

Daddy registered me for classes at the Art Students' League, where Zorach himself taught. It was early May. My father, speaking in his familiar voice—intimate, humorous—said he was leaving the city but would be back in a couple of weeks. Would I be all right? He gave me a handful of cash—"For buttons and lunch," he said.

After he had left, I found a case of beer in a closet. Each night I drank one bottle and listened to the radio. A man named Long John came on at midnight. Between recordings of hit songs, he told hard-luck stories about rural people who came to the city for what he called "the big life."

A Tennessee family had come by train along with a coffin in the baggage car containing their dead grandmother. They were drifting around Pennsylvania Station. Having heard about him down on the farm, they telephoned Long John. He asked listeners to come to the broadcasting station and bring money.

I listened to him every night, and then I listened to "The Star-Spangled Banner" until the last note had sounded.

Zorach's classroom smelled powerfully of the damp clay stored there in large vats. Our model, a heavy redheaded woman, stood on a dais, naked. After a few days, Zorach walked over to me and looked at what I'd done. "You have a wild talent," he said, as though he were making a pronouncement on Sinai.

On days when there was no class, I went to two or three movies in succession. I ate at a Horn and Hardart cafeteria nearby. Something attracted me about the glass boxes that held sandwiches and pieces of cake.

Then I ran out of money. I began to model—for Zorach, for a muralist, and for a Japanese painter.

When Miriam, a fellow student, suggested I do commercial modeling, I confessed I had nothing to wear. She gave me a cotton plaid dress smocked at the waist and loaned me a polo coat. I had my own saddle shoes. We found the name of a modeling agency in the telephone book.

I had a long wait in the office of the Grey Agency, where sleek, pretty young women also waited, large black portfolios at their feet. Unlike me, they were all appropriately dressed, a lesson in clothes I absorbed at once.

At last I was ushered into the inner office of a woman who was not pretty but all business. She asked me to pull up my skirt so she could look at my legs. After I'd complied, I was required to lean over and sweep my hair forward so she could see my neck.

She consulted a wallboard covered with slips of paper, each with a written address. "You'll need to hurry," she said, after giving me directions and one of the slips.

The place was a town house off Madison Avenue, midtown. I looked past open doors at a marble floor covered with black cables. Men walked about among cameras on tripods, occasionally bending to look through a lens. One of them saw me and smiled.

I couldn't do it; I didn't have the nerve. I left. The man who had smiled at me ran out of the town house. I looked down at the sidewalk while he tried to persuade me to come back, make up my face, wear the dresses piled on a couch, and pose for them.

The thought of it in the days that followed was nearly intolerable. I had had a chance. I blew it.

My father ultimately returned. It might have been late spring. He made arrangements for Miriam—who had become my friend—and me to go to Nantucket for several months, an island where I had spent a week with my grandmother a few years earlier.

Like many of Daddy's arrangements, it started with an impulse. He paid our fares for the ferry and what he guessed would be a few months' rent and living expenses. The money covered one month.

We found a two-room cottage in Siasconset. The front door, somewhat lopsided on its hinges, opened to a street that glared with the whiteness of crushed oyster shells. The two rooms were crowded with shabby furniture and a seriously out-of-tune upright piano. But the rooms smelled cleanly of the sea. At the back of the cottage, a path wound among little gray-shingled houses, their fences covered with rambler roses that bloomed soon after we moved in.

One evening as Miriam and I played a Scarlatti duet, badly, she with violin and me at the piano, a thin young man stepped through an open window, weeping and almost incoherent.

We made out that the cause of his grief was that European churches would be destroyed by bombs if there was a war. And there would be one! Think of the marvelous stained-glass windows! Their destruction was inevitable.

We commiserated with him, reminded him that whole populations would die too, and after an hour or so he left as he'd arrived, through the window.

We found jobs, Miriam as a waitress in a restaurant that opened in May, me as an errand girl for the 'Sconset summer theater group. I made a friend, Jon, among the actors. We swam together in the late afternoons if he wasn't in rehearsal. Morgan, the director of the group, asked me if I wanted to be an extra in a play by Thornton Wilder, *Our Town,* a nameless mourner at the funeral of the lead character. I was provided with a costume, an umbrella, and a place to stand.

On opening night, Katherine Cornell and her husband, Guthrie McClintock, had come from Martha's Vineyard especially to watch a young actress in the cast, Ruth March.

I stood with my back to the audience, beneath the umbrella, which was open because the play called for rain. If

I looked to the left, I could see Jon facing me, half hidden by the curtain. He began to make funny faces. Since mirth was out of place unless called for, and especially at a funeral, it was doubly irresistible. The stage was flooded with my laughter, the auditorium itself, and the ears of the two distinguished guests. My career in the theater ended at the moment it began.

But Morgan continued to take long walks by the ocean with me. He didn't reproach me for the night of the big laugh—though the curtain was lowered briefly when it was apparent that I couldn't stop—I went on being an errand girl for the company.

One morning, at dawn, I put on my bathing suit. So as not to wake Miriam, I crept silently out of the little house.

'Sconset sat snugly on the edge of a bluff down which wooden stairs led to the beach. As I stood on the top step, the sun was rising on the horizon. I looked down at the still-shadowed shacks on the sand where, in some of them, the servants of the summer people lived. It was called Codfish Park.

All at once, a few black women began to emerge from the shacks. They wore white robes that billowed as they seemed to float toward the sea like so many white and black blossoms blown by a dawn wind.

During the months I spent on Nantucket, I was courted by a Harvard freshman and a high school teacher from New Jersey who drank too much. The freshman had an older brother whose face appeared to swell every time he looked at me, though he never spoke a word.

One evening after dark, the teacher and I set out across the golf course. The rotating Tom Nevers light, our destination, poked at the sea with its broad finger, then at the small rises and dips of the course, light without end.

We stumbled on a sand trap. He nearly dropped the gin drink he'd carried from the bar where we had met earlier. I hadn't meant to say that I loved him. I didn't. But the three words had risen, flooded my mouth, poured out. He was in any event too drunk to respond. And I was too puzzled and mortified to repeat the words. So I threw them away for a long time.

My grandmother had told me that her husband, on one of his many visits to the United States, had taken a boat from New York City to Nantucket long before most of the houses in 'Sconset had been built. When I imagined him there, he was dressed like a Spanish dancer, standing on the bluff, looking out to sea. A fierce wind blew yet did not dislodge his flat black dancer's hat.

At the end of our fourth month on the island, I heard from my father that I would be going to a Canadian boarding school in September. I returned to Kew Gardens, where I stayed with my grandmother. I felt bleakly grateful for not having to go back to the Syrian's West Side apartment where I had spent such desolate days and nights.

My grandmother asked me to visit my mother before I went off to Canada. A thrill of fear went through me. Yet I was powerfully drawn to Elsie, who had formed my first sense of the world by a refusal so absolute that one of its consequences was that she seemed neither male nor female to me, a genderless presence who must be propitiated, but always in vain.

The same day, I went to see my father, who was staying in Mary's Greenwich Village apartment on Charles Street. He gave me "a piece of change" to buy Elsie freesias and arrowroot biscuits, for both of which she had what he characterized as intense greediness.

When I came to her door, holding the bouquet of freesias and the biscuits, I stood in front of it without knocking, rehearsing what I was going to say. But she suddenly opened the door. "I thought it was you," she said, with a smile.

Daddy had said she was living with an editor from a New York publishing house. My father called him "an old sheet from Sheet Harbour," because he had been born in a town of that name on Nova Scotia.

I had not been alone with her since we had bought shoes in De Pinna's, other than in the bathroom of Mary's Florida house. I could hear the strain in her voice as she tried to fill in silences. I strained too, to respond, to react. In what I judged to be a burst of artificial intimacy, she told me a story that illustrated her jealousy. She acknowledged that trait as though it were a peculiarly Spanish virtue.

She and the editor, Harmon, had had a fight, which had ended temporarily with his leaving the apartment in a rage. The first thing she did was to find his address book and send telegrams to everyone listed in it. "I'm in desperate trouble. Can you send me two dollars?"

She laughed as she told me Harmon was very "tight with money" and the telegrams had humiliated him. Another time, suspecting that he was having an affair with someone, she had taken his underwear to a pharmacist to have the stains analyzed.

I had a revelation. She was pleading with me to be recognized, not as my mother but as an entertainer. The first story had evoked my laughter, but not the second.

I asked her how she had met my father. "He and Leopold were in the navy together," she replied. "One day Leopold brought him home to us. We all fell for him, my brothers, my mother, and me. But I was in love with a Jewish student at Columbia University. Paul wrote scenes for me to play with Harold, who didn't love me back. They were pretty good scenes. I recall how we walked on upper Broadway, your father and I, working out ways I could get Harold involved with me." She smiled as though forgiving herself for an indiscretion.

She didn't refer in any way to the telephone call she had made to Florida and our conversation. She appeared to have forgotten it. I hadn't, or the question she asked me during it: Did I love her? Her tone had been utterly assured. She had never doubted it. In some way I did love her, if an intense preoccupation with someone is love.

At some point that afternoon, Dina, her dachshund, trotted into the room, wagging her tail. "Did you know you can embarrass a dachshund?" she asked me. I shook my head. Her voice grew deeper, reproachful, as she looked at the dog and spoke. "Why, Dina! How could you! Such a bad little dachshund!" And Dina began to lick herself, stopped, looked guilty, yawned. My mother laughed. "All right, Dina, it's over," she said, clapping her hands.

Mary took me shopping; she bought several things at Bonwit Teller's. When she paid for them, she bent down and took off one shoe, where she kept money. My father had told me she was eccentric.

Montréal

Sainte-Geneviève was a small finishing school in Montréal. I spent nearly a year in its rambling four-story house, September to mid-July.

After dinner, those of us who boarded were obliged to play bridge. Madame Duvernoy, who taught French and comportment, changed tables each night. There were eleven boarders, and she made the twelth bridge player.

Everyone dreaded to have her for a partner. She held her cards close to her face in small fat hands that were like faded pink mittens. She was drunk every evening. Her marceled hair was unmoving, like a cap. She would purse her thickly rouged lips just before she made an impossible bid. If her partner groaned or laughed out loud, Madame Duvernoy smiled enigmatically.

Afterward, when we went to our rooms in the old house, which was a block or so from one of the main streets, Sherbrooke Avenue, we had savage conversations about sex. Did old people in their forties do it? The bedroom of the headmistress, Madame Chennoux, who owned the school, and her husband, a lawyer, was on the second floor. She was at least fifty. Still, we took turns listening at her door in the middle of the night, hoping, dreading, to overhear some intimacy. Her husband was shorter than she was, a fact that added a further dimension to the grotesque stories we invented about the carnal life of the grown-ups among whom we lived, compliant young girls with hearts of ice.

Most of the students were fifteen or sixteen, the rest, a year or two older. The blondes among us were covered with a fine down only visible in sunlight; the brunettes decried the dark springing hairs on their arms and legs that intimated hidden thickets which, one of us had read in a prohibited book, only whores shaved away.

Two of the girls, it was rumored among us, had no interest in boys. They smiled sardonically at our preoccupation with them. We whispered to close friends our thoughts about these girls—that they entertained each other all night long and urinated like men, standing up. One of them had the face of a pug dog and wore around her wrist a broad leather strap with a silver buckle. She was an outstanding student, but she learned derisively, as though conceding to a madness in adults that drove them to teach.

She was a skilled pianist. She played Chopin's "Revolutionary Étude" with such intensity it seemed that an army was about to storm the house. What we most admired her for was her imitation of Madame Duvernoy, dead drunk, playing bridge, becoming slowly aware she had forgotten to dress and was, in fact, stark naked.

We found sex in everything. We each had to plan and cook an entire dinner once during the term. We laughed insanely at the Mont Blanc I made with its nippled peak of whipped cream, at the leg of lamb reclining on a bed of flageolets that was like, someone said, the bluish splotchy thigh of an elderly man, and at the lewd rigidity of the root vegetables I had chosen as side dishes.

One of the girls, Moira, suddenly announced she was leaving the school to get married. It happened so quickly! In a week! We were thunderstruck. But it turned out that she was not pregnant as we had been sure she was.

Toward the end of the school year, she came to visit the school. We were mute, staring at her. She had been "doing it" all these months! Surely there would be a sign! To everyone's surprise, she appeared unchanged, perhaps slightly more sedate than we had remembered.

My father came to see me around Easter. Although—as I was mortified to learn—he didn't pay school bills on time, he bought me a small luxurious case of Elizabeth Arden cosmetics. My room-mate, Dorothy, who was from El Paso, and I used up the creams in a week. In certain moods, we wanted to be like the courtesans we read about in Balzac.

My father tried to seduce Dorothy, who was six feet tall with a small square jaw and a tremulous voice. When she told me about it, I couldn't look at her. My own father!

When? I asked her. When I had gone to use the bathroom in his hotel room before he took us out to dinner, she said. But I hadn't been gone more than two minutes! What could he have done in that time?

"He looked at me in a certain way . . . he whispered," she said. Whispered! What did he whisper? She couldn't make it out, she said. "But I know it was about *it*." She giggled then and observed that all men were alike, even fathers.

Even, probably, the Franciscan brothers in their brown habits who walked on the streets of Montréal, wearing sandals on their feet in all kinds of weather.

Several of us went out with McGill boys. We returned from our trysts with lips and breasts sore, eyes glazed, breath caught between appalled laughter and tears.

My best friend, Claudia, a day student, was rich and glamorous and wore thick black mascara that took her half an hour to brush on. One day she told me she had been "doing it" for nearly six months. She lit a cigarette and began to tell me details until I made her stop. I glimpsed her boyfriend once or twice, a French Canadian as sleek as a greyhound.

On winter weekends, we went to a ski cabin in the Laurentian Mountains. During one of them, a day student, Penelope, and I got hold of a gallon of red wine made by the local people in Sainte-Adèle. All of them wore wigs and didn't have an eyebrow or an eyelash among them. Their hairlessness, it was rumored, was a result of hereditary syphilis.

We drank all the wine and were violently sick a few minutes

later. We couldn't play bridge because we were far drunker than we'd ever known Madame Duvorney to be. Madame Chennoux treated us as tenderly as babies but repeated in her dry austere way that she hoped we'd learned a serious lesson for the future.

Another boarder had mentioned a novel, *Sons and Lovers* by D. H. Lawrence. The title promised wantonness and scandal. I found a copy among the books in the Sainte-Geneviève library.

As I read the novel, I sank into the world of Paul Morel. The text ignited a latent sense in me of the desirability of self-knowledge. There were other realities in life beside my own. I had not really thought about my life. I began to glimpse at the most elementary level fragments of my own reality. The novel calmed my turbulence, eased my restlessness and shame.

One evening in early December, Madame Chennoux answered a ring at the front door. I was playing bridge, facing the hall. Three people stood on the threshold, a middle-aged woman, a young athletic-looking man, and a girl around my own age. Madame's face grew stern when she was introduced to the young man, but she was welcoming to the girl and gripped her hand firmly. I knew she was to be a boarder in the school.

Gilberte had long dark lank hair that curled at the ends like notes on a music staff. I imagined her in a flash, winding her hair on rollers as she stood in the room of a run-down hotel. The mother and daughter looked shabby, somewhat run-down themselves. The daughter was dressed like a tart, in a mangy fur shrug that gave her a hunched look. She wore a tight black skirt that wrinkled over her rear end. Her face was small and sharp-jawed. She had huge dazed dark eyes.

Madame called me and asked me to show Gilberte up to the third floor; she was to occupy a third bed in the room I shared with Dorothy. As she walked up the stairs sideways, she lit a cigarette. She was carrying a small worn suitcase with someone else's initials on it. An antenna in me reached out and sensed her beggarliness, her forlorn life. I began to detest her.

But she clung to me. Her face was always damp, as though she leaked tears through her skin. She confided in me, in a flat nasal voice, that her parents were divorced, that she had been sent to many schools in France, that the young athletic man lived with her mother.

She was given to momentary fits of anger over trivial things, involuntary anger like that of a small animal misreading signs and feeling under attack. She recognized in me another nomad.

Moments before we boarders went into a theater to see a performance of *Tobit and the Angel*, she handed me, awkwardly, a Christmas present, a box of heavily scented bath powder.

"Flour!" I exclaimed, upon opening it during an intermission. Several of my schoolmates laughed. I glimpsed Gilberte's face, turned toward me a few seats away like tallow glowing in the shadows, and felt a corrosive guilt.

My friend Penelope, whose father was a McGill university professor, lived in a tall house on the campus. It was furnished in a spartan but comfortable fashion. The family—mother, father, and daughter—conveyed an atmosphere of amiability and unaffected learning. I spent hours in their house, most of them in Penelope's bedroom, which was barely furnished except for an elaborate dressing table with carved drawers and a triple mirror. I was at ease with Penny. I had made silence a test. We could read our books in the same room without having to speak. And we had sinned together: we were hors de combat, as Madame Chennoux said of our weekend spree and its consequence.

A McGill freshman, Robert, asked me to the St. Andrew's Ball. I was half mad with anxiety. I had no evening gown.

There was a third American at Sainte-Geneviève, a debutante from Long Island who wore her blond hair like a half veil over her face. When I asked if I might borrow one of her three evening gowns, she stared at me silently from her bed, holding a book in the air. She dropped it and pressed a finger into her cheek, depressing the skin. Then she rose and went to her closet and flung open the door.

I saw a hat on a shelf; its brim was covered with small

silky-looking brown and beige feathers. Below the shelf hung blouses, skirts, and dresses and one full-length white fox-fur coat. She had returned to her bed and was watching me. I chose one of the gowns, determined to wear it however it looked. I took it from its hanger and, carrying it like a body, smiled in her direction, not meeting her eyes.

That night, in a corridor of the Ritz Hotel where the ball was held, bagpipers played their bagpipes, marching back and forth, their plaid skirts swinging, revealing their strong legs and hairy knees. The governor general of Canada, John Buchan, given the honorary title of Lord Tweedsmuir, made a speech, but no one I glanced at was listening. There was such excitement, such anticipation, in the air. Robert and I danced for hours until the corsage of wild orchids he had given me drooped and I dropped it in a basket. Then we left the Ritz and walked along the street that led to Mont Royal. From the heights we looked down at the city. We kissed, grew aware of other people standing near, left. We halted on the long flight of stairs down, kissed again and again.

I got back to Sainte-Geneviève as the sky was growing pale with dawn. Madame Chennoux let me in, wearing a robe, a plait of her gray hair hanging down her back. We stood in the dark hall while she decided not to punish me. She asked me how the evening had been. I gave her a not-quite-full report. She kept her eyes from the dress, which she must have known was borrowed.

When I returned it, it seemed possessed by a devil. The narrow shoulder straps slid off the hanger. When I straightened them, the skirt ballooned, and as I pushed the skirt back into the closet, the straps slid again, just as its owner entered the room. She took the dress from me and, with a grim face, hung it with dismissive efficiency next to the other gowns.

I thanked her for the loan of the dress, again without looking at her directly, this time to hide the triumph I was feeling and that I feared would show on my face. She hadn't been asked to the ball.

Madame Chennoux belonged to the Oxford Movement for Moral Rearmament. Every school morning, she came to the living room before our French class began with Madame Duvernoy, to give us a brief talk on honesty, unselfishness, and social usefulness. Her fine head, covered with silver hair, and her noble profile made me think of eagles. She squinted every so often and gazed down at her thin hands.

Once, glimpsing my reflection in the night-black window of the ski train we rode to the mountains, she murmured, "My lion . . . ."

She had a cross-eyed Irish setter she took on long snow walks there.

When she returned to our weekend cabin and spoke to us, I detected a slight tremor of her head. I attributed it to the intensity of her convictions.

* * *

A redheaded girl from Toronto, a boarder at the school, knitted angora sweaters throughout our classes. She often waved her hands wildly to rid her fingers of the clinging wool, squeezing her eyes shut and making a *poof* sound with her pursed lips. Then her usual tranquil expression returned to her face—until the next battle with wool. The room is always sunny in memory, though it must have rained and snowed some days. Beneath the knitter's long fingers, white angora wool became a sweater. She wore a pink one she had made.

One of the maids whose features instantly come to mind was named Marie. She was narrow-faced, and her voice was friendly but wary. She would announce telephone calls, and one of us would get up to take the call in the hallway.

A figure appears to me; it seems to cling to the phone. It's hard to make out the features, but I can sense a smile, hear low laughter. The call is from a boyfriend. It is always brief. She usually ends it . . . goodbye, goodbye . . . she is thinking of her dinner growing cold.

I meet Robert in the bar of a hotel on Sherbrooke Avenue. We order Canadian Club highballs. I feel elegant, luxurious, although everything I have on is borrowed except for my shoes, even the little hat with the dotted black veil.

At the last moment, the boarders gone, I received a note from my father inviting me to spend the school's Christmas holiday, half over by then, on Prince Edward Island, where Mary, now his wife, had bought or rented a house.

I took a train to Moncton, then a ferry that crossed Northumberland Strait to Borden, where Daddy met the boat. We greeted each other. I was cautious from habit, my pleasure at seeing him tainted with defensiveness.

But this time he was defensive, too, and edgy. I noted a long white box, the kind used for floral deliveries, lying on the back seat of the car.

He spoke about a cleaning woman Mary employed who came twice a week to the house we were driving toward. He changed the subject: How was the trip from Montréal? he asked, then abruptly interrupted himself to tell me to take the cover from the box.

Inside there was a silver fox fur. "Trapped on the island," he said, as though that made it more valuable. Should he give it to the cleaning woman? Or me?

I wanted the fur. I felt a blush flaring. I suggested there might not be any place on the island where a woman could wear the fur, but in Montréal it wouldn't be out of place.

A memory slid into my mind. It was about Daddy and Vin Lawrence from Hollywood days. Early in the morning, after a night of drinking, both of them sick from alcoholic excess, they had stumbled into a Los Angeles cafeteria. They looked like bums. I didn't recall whose idea it was to measure the waitress's charity by asking for free cups of coffee, but it was an irresistible impulse. If the waitress took pity on them, they'd give her $100. If she didn't, they would pay for the coffee and leave, but not before letting her know what she had lost.

Wasn't this a similar test? The hell with it, I told myself. I'd take the fur.

I knew I had failed when I saw his slow, sardonic smile.

"Merry Christmas," he said.

A few days before or after Christmas, I went to a party with the housekeeper's younger brother. We traveled to a remote hamlet on the island by sleigh. It was drawn by a black horse, the bells on his harness ringing out as we went through woods and fields covered with snow that gave off a white radiance. We paused briefly at a little house where an elderly couple, acquaintances of the boy, had given themselves one Christmas present, a small organ. Neither could play. I offered to play a few chords and, while I did, I could hear sighs of pleasure.

A few minutes later, we arrived at a dimly lit grange hall, a few cabins crouching around it. Inside, a big black stove sent out waves of intense heat, which didn't reach to the end of two long benches. Boys and men sat on one side, girls and women on the other. An old fiddler and a young accordion player on a low platform made hectic music. Every so often, a couple got up to dance boisterously.

The island was dry; you could only buy liquor at government stores. The boys kept going outside to drink from little bottles of vanilla extract and to write their names on the snow with their urine. There was much raucous laughter and snow-muffled scuffling outside the door.

Later, when the housekeeper's brother and I reached home, he showed me a photograph of one of his sisters. She was wearing black underwear. I started to smile, then saw by the proud expression on his face that it would be a mistake. She had run away to Montréal but had made a big success there. Did I know her? he asked. I hadn't run into her, I answered.

Daddy and Mary read aloud to each other from Boswell's *Life of Johnson* during the long winter evenings. From time to time, they would laugh in a way I thought to be worldly and desirable.

After the presents were opened Christmas morning, Daddy began to drink steadily, muttering about the anticlimax of Christmas afternoons, when the light was always dreary and dull and time moved sluggishly. How he hated it all! Scrooge was a betrayer of his class, and everything about the holiday was designed to bring out the worst in people.

One morning I looked into the room he used for a study. He was asleep on the couch. When I told him later, he said, "I was thinking, pal." He mocked himself as well as me.

I wondered about that but soon forgot whatever conclusion I came to. He began to tell me a theater story.

John Barrymore had the lead in one of Shakespeare's plays, I forget which. He was the king. When he died, he was placed on a bier onstage. One of his courtiers, wearing a long false beard, bent over his king's dead armored body and spoke a few words in formal farewell. Barrymore moved ever so slightly. His helmet caught the tip of the beard. The actor had either to stand up straight, ripping off his beard, or run alongside the bier as it was carried offstage. He did the latter, improvising on Shakespeare as he ran.

I had confessed to my father that I had a secret passion for the actor Franchot Tone. On the day I was to return to Montréal, Daddy took me to a diner in Summerside where a Chinese waiter brought our order. I liked looking at him. My father noticed and called him "Franchot Wong."

The ferryboat wasn't running that day. I had to fly. Daddy drove me to the small island airport where I climbed into the two-seated plane that would take me to Moncton. The water was frozen. When I looked down at it, the ice glittered like a vast field of fool's gold. I looked at the head of the pilot, all I could see of him, and wished the flight could go on forever.

During the one-week spring break, I took the train to New York City and saw my father again. He had come from

Canada on publishing business, he told me. I stayed with my grandmother in Kew Gardens and went by subway into the city every day.

On one of those days, shortly after noon, I found myself in a long queue of tearful, noisy girls outside the Paramount Theater box office, where the new Franchot Tone movie was playing.

The Paramount still had stage shows. I hadn't heard of Frank Sinatra, but when a thin, bony, hollow-cheeked young man appeared on stage, the audience, mostly female, exploded in screams and sobs. He began to sing, accompanied by the sustained wailing of the undone girls. I had come to worship. What they were there for, I didn't know.

I spent my return train fare on a dress I found in Altman's. Those were the days when you could return a garment even after a week or more as long as it wasn't torn or dirty. I planned to wear it to a Group Theater production of an Irwin Shaw play, *The Gentle People*, and return the dress the following day. Franchot Tone was playing the lead. I noticed I attracted a good deal of attention as I walked down the theater aisle that night. Later, I found a large rectangular price tag safety-pinned to the back of the dress.

My father had gotten the ticket for me from Walter Fried, the Group Theater business manager. He knew him from the time he had been involved with the Provincetown Theater on Cape Cod. At that same time, Eugene O'Neill was writing one-act plays to be presented by the theater, and Bert Lahr could be spotted walking on Commercial Street, on his way to a morning rehearsal, wearing his green beret.

During intermission, I found Fried—or Uncle Wally, as my father called him—sitting in the box office, wearing his black fedora aslant and smoking a thin cigar. He said he had made an arrangement for me to meet the cast in a bar across the street.

When the play ended, I went to the bar, the price tag still hanging from the dress. Members of the cast began to drift in, but Tone didn't show up.

I thought it was a trick of Uncle Wally's. In any event, actually meeting the actor would have been painful if thrilling. When I got back to Kew Gardens, I found the exposed price tag. That would have made the meeting doubly mortifying.

On the last afternoon of spring vacation, my father took me to see the movie *Grand Illusion*. The splendor of the movie made up for nearly everything, even the price tag on the dress. He had already seen it. In the pale light cast onto the audience from the screen, he was watching me. I sensed he wanted to see how I reacted. I had begun by then to notice an impulse in him—noble, he would have called it in someone else—to teach. And as a teacher, he always was running out of time, with one more thing to impart about literature and films before he left.

*　*　*

At the end of May and early June, the boarding students left Sainte-Geneviève. Madame Chennoux couldn't reach my father by telephone or telegram. He didn't get in touch with the school until the beginning of July to make arrangements for me to go to Halifax, Nova Scotia.

Perhaps to console me for being the last student left, Madame Duvernoy took me to a concert. It was given a few days before she was to leave for a holiday in France, where she had relatives living in Lyon.

In the middle of the Brahms Piano Concerto in B Flat, a short man in a shabby brown suit raced down the central aisle of the concert hall, his hands waving frantically in the air. He clambered up to the podium, grabbed the conductor's arm with great force, and whispered in his ear. The music ceased.

"La France a capitulée!" the short man shouted, as he stared down at us all. Madame Duvernoy turned to me. Her hands flew to cover her ears, and there was an expression of horror on her face. It was June 22, 1940.

We spent three weeks in Nova Scotia in a woebegone little house whose front door opened to within a few yards of a twenty-foot bluff. A dusty train banged and rattled through the backyard twice a day on its way to and from Lunenberg, a nearby fishing town. A local woman came to clean the house twice a week, and there was a nearby village where we could buy groceries.

Except for the few days in Florida, it was the longest time I spent alone with my father. By the end of the first few days, he had gotten to know nearly everyone in the village, and we weren't often by ourselves.

He and the local minister introduced me to fishing for salmon in a wide stream. He gave me a few shooting lessons, which drew the attention of a Canadian Mountie, first to the rifle we had used and then to me. His resplendent uniform gave him an air of gravity and the law, but he shed both in the kitchen, where he offered to show Daddy the location of various illegal whiskey stills.

That evening, accompanied by the Mountie out of uniform, we stopped by a few of them, and my father had some samples. Then, with the Mountie at the wheel of our car, we went to a billiard parlor in Halifax.

In a back room, plump middle-aged local women cavorted like aproned elephants. The laughter was strident, and my father, close to passing out, crawled around on the floor, barking like a dog. The Mountie and I stood behind one of the two billiard tables in the front room, I watching my father with anguished helplessness, the Mountie watching me with what Daddy had characterized as "hot" eyes.

The next morning, Daddy awoke, ashen-faced and weak. He had, he said, "the humblies," and would I shave him? He struggled to get into the bathtub and lie down in his sour-smelling clothes while I did my best with the razor.

Afterward, when he looked in the small bathroom mirror,

stretching out his chin to see what I had wrought, he seemed to catch sight of himself, lurching through his days and nights. He was silent most of that day, grim and depleted.

But the next day his mood changed. He recited bits of poetry: " 'Ah, yesternight, betwixt the roses and the wine, there fell thy shadow, Cynara, and I was desolate and sick of an old passion.' " I responded by quoting Tennyson: " 'Come into the garden, Maud,/ For the black bat, night—' " and he said, with comical emphasis, "I'll Maud you, you little spic." And so it went on, he irreverent, I laughing helplessly.

He told me bits of gossip, fragments of what he considered wisdom: Men fight wars to get new women; actresses always fall for the clowns. Gabriele D'Annunzio took a lobster for a walk, a green ribbon attached to its claw; Charles Laughton and Elsa Lanchester had married each other to disguise their homosexuality. When Laughton grew tired on the set of whatever movie he was making, my father said he began to camp. I asked him what that meant, and he replied that it was a way of exaggerating and at the same time mocking the female side of one's nature.

I wondered if Leopold camped. But Daddy said Leopold was a Spanish puritan and punished himself for his homosexuality by devising an agonizing condition for himself, tic douloureux.

He continued the long lesson that had begun in Peterborough: economy of effort. Instead of making a number of trips about the kitchen, he taught me to bring together everything I needed before I began a task: soap, scouring brush, drying towel. It was the only kind of order I saw in him.

Toward the end of the last week, we had a serious quarrel. I have forgotten the cause, but I recall the occasion. We were sitting in a rigid wooden swing connected at the top with two slanted benches across from each other.

Suddenly I called him a third-rate writer. I regretted it instantly when I looked up at his face. We were each other's prisoners in the swing. He held it still and stepped out and went into the house. I had wounded him in the only way I could think of.

We packed up the car, Daddy adding to the top of the luggage a tricycle for the housekeeper's son, whom she had spoken of often, referring to him as "little Johnny." She was coming the next day to clean up the house.

On our way to the Boston-bound ferryboat, we stopped by the hamlet where the housekeeper lived to drop off the tricycle. As we parked, she appeared on the porch, behind her a dwarf who looked at least thirty. She clasped her hands then waved at us, while little Johnny ran down the walk to claim his gift.

We drove away, both of us appalled and bursting with laughter at the misunderstanding. In the midst of merriment, we forgave each other for what had happened between us in the wooden swing.

Later, I had to use a bathroom. He said we could stop at anyone's house. I protested that I couldn't ask strangers for such an intimate favor, I'd just hold it. He finally persuaded me, saying he'd be "charming." I said, "Don't be too damned charming!" That amused him more than the dwarf and the tricycle.

New York City

Daddy took me to the Barbizon Hotel, in those days a female-only accommodation in New York City.

He stood at the registration desk, smiling at the woman clerk, ready to oblige her in any way he could, presenting himself as the spirit of geniality, still handsome, though alcohol had begun to erode his face. She gave him a form. He took out a pen as he looked it over; he found a snag. The hotel required someone to vouch for me besides him.

But as was usual then, he had a solution for any problem. He had said to me that if I ever needed him, to send him a telegram: SEND OUT THE TROOPS.

He telephoned a cousin I'd not met, Faith Baldwin, in her Connecticut home. She refused to vouch for me. Instead, she lectured him about the perils of my staying in a hotel at my age. It was a long lecture. He hung up the telephone, and we slunk away from the hotel desk.

Years later, a good friend said to me of Faith Baldwin's novels, "When you've read them all, you've read one."

* * *

Daddy performed what seemed a miracle. He got me into the Juilliard School of Music, then on Claremont Avenue near 115th Street. The same day he registered me at International House, a large hostel for various students, many of them foreigners.

He was skilled at lying to officials and in elaborating hugely on a theme as small as a grain of rice. I never heard remorse in his voice. But I didn't hear self-admiration either. My father lacked the vanity side of pride; he made fun of it, saying the human animal had nothing to be proud of.

I once lied when I accompanied my cousin Natalie to her convent school to pick up her homework, which she'd forgotten to take home. A nun asked if I was a Catholic. I said yes. When she left the small anteroom where I waited for Natalie, I picked up a booklet that featured lurid drawings of hell. One crudely drawn scene depicted bodies toasting like marshmallows over flames—the punishment for liars.

Juilliard was threaded by white corridors along which were practice rooms. The muffled sounds of the various instruments made a blurred, discordant rumble and squeak unless you were in one of the soundproof rooms. There were also classrooms where one could study music theory and harmonics, and a small theater in which the students gave concerts.

I went several days a week and took lessons on the piano

in a windowless, claustrophobic room, its space dominated by the black wing and keyboard of a much-used baby grand.

I had moved my scant wardrobe into one of the rooms in the female section of International House and on my first day found a kind of louche society there, or so it might have seemed to an outsider.

The toothless younger son of the owner of a chain of clothing stores played chess with me; an adolescent piano student, Paul, from El Paso, became a friend; a small plump Spaniard studying hotel management, a subject also pursued by all the Swiss students at the House, spoke Spanish with me and made me laugh with jokes characterized by Spanish irony and its almost exalted irritability.

Then there was Burl Ives, who had a weekly radio program on which he sang folk songs and played his guitar. He was a big red-headed man, kindly, except when he got into a barroom brawl, which he did regularly. One evening he cried out in the cafeteria, "I hear them snakes hollering out on Riverside Drive tonight," and beckoned to me.

We took a taxi to the radio station and drove there through Central Park. He played his guitar and sang for the driver and for me in his light, mellow tenor. We arrived at the station with two minutes to spare before his broadcast.

Mary paid for singing lessons. My teacher, Harriet, lived on the top floor of a Riverside Drive apartment house. One night I stayed for supper, and although the singing teacher's face has faded from memory, I can still see her plump adolescent son, dressed in a kilt, piping in each supper course she brought us. It mortified me, though I can't think why. Perhaps I imagined Elsie was watching us with her magic telescope.

Elsie told me about a wealthy South American relative from Colombia staying for a few weeks in his Sutton Place apartment, a kind of pied-à-terre. Although I was unaware of the desperation that drove me to telephone him, of its force in my life, its contamination of nearly every feeling I had, I convinced myself it would be a joke to meet him. I would make a story of the visit to tell people—and myself. After all, I would hear it too.

He sent a black limousine to International House for me. It was not the enormously lengthened sort of limo that howls throughout its swollen length of the wealth and celebrity of the passenger. It was a more mannered cry.

My cousin lived on a high floor. While I was visiting, he made a series of telephone calls, to Paris, Berlin, and London. While he was speaking to London, I heard the clanging of Big Ben's clock as it rang out the hour. He showed me a few gold artifacts, most of them elaborate nipple covers that resembled thimbles, discovered in the darkest recesses of his mine by his workers. They were thousands of years old. Shortly after, he brought me a dish of dried fruit. When I said no-thank-you, he speculated aloud about whether or not I enjoyed sex.

I left shortly, and though he offered me the black limousine to go back to International House, I said no to that, too.

I saw my mother twice during the autumn I was a Juilliard student. I can't imagine that she requested my company; I must have gone to see her on my own the first time.

"Come in, Paula," I hear her say, a half century later. It sounded to me then as if she'd said, "Go away, Paula."

Was it she who always imposed a painful formality between us? Or by then was it a collaboration of the two of us? As some people are inclined to do in such tense circumstances, she simulated frankness and told me personal stories about herself, more detailed perhaps than she intended, or else a certain brutal self-revelation was her specialty. Perhaps she didn't know any better.

She smoked constantly, lighting one cigarette from the end of another.

The second time I saw her was when I was taken by taxi to her apartment accompanied by my El Paso friend, Paul, and another acquaintance from International House. My face was red with fever. She was expecting me. Friends had telephoned her to tell her that I was ill. They half carried me up the stairs.

When she opened the door, I saw she was dressed in a coat. An open sack of oranges sat on a table. She waited until my friends had gone and then said to me politely, "Take care of yourself," and left. Harmon was gone too. I spent the night there.

Perhaps to atone for what even I could judge as utter neglect, she invited me a few weeks later to a concert conducted by Arturo Toscanini. I had a date with a Columbia University medical student. I told her I had an engagement that night. "Engagement?" she asked lightly, with sardonic disbelief.

My life was incoherent to me. I felt it quivering, spitting out broken teeth. When I thought of the purposes I had tried to find for myself the last year, to show my father that I "wanted" something—piano, voice lessons, sculpture, none of the least use to me—when I thought of the madness of my parents where I was concerned, I felt the bleakest misery.

A middle-aged woman named Kay, an acquaintance of Mary's, lived on the other side of the Susquehanna River across from Mary's cousins, Henry and Baby.

Her life had unraveled. She was giving a few piano lessons to a few children, and playing the Ouija board to encourage in her a sense that she had a fate. My father persuaded her to take me to California. I never doubted my father's powers of persuasion.

Mary bought us a second-hand convertible Chevrolet and gave Kay some money. One winter morning the two of us, lots of Kay's luggage, and her little dog set out for the long drive that getting to California entailed in those days. At least, in that rakish little car, we didn't look like refugees from *Tobacco Road*.

California

The first day, I discovered Kay was an alcoholic and that most of the driving would have to be done by me. Drunk or sober, depending on whether we'd stopped at any roadside taverns, she took what she called "monkey glands." They were good, she said, to help delay the ravages of age. She talked in fits and starts, first voluble, then silent for hours. From gnatlike clusters of words, I gathered that she knew Delores Del Rio and some of the Barrymore family.

Now and then she had me stop the car in empty stretches of road so she could get out, fall to her knees, and pray to whatever god she had momentary faith in.

We stopped in Dallas and I telephoned my roommate, Dorothy, from Sainte-Geneviève. She was astonished to hear my voice. I arranged to meet her that evening, along with her brother, at a nightclub. I left a sodden Kay in a small hotel on the outskirts of the city.

There was a dance contest in the club, and I won the second prize. An ancient lady, the sentimental favorite with the patrons, won the first, dancing a waltz with a professional dancer hired for the occasion.

Then the spotlight fell upon me. People applauded. I stood up and walked toward the pro. He whispered fiercely to me as we tangoed—"Turn now! Left! Right! Backward dip!"—while he beamed at the audience. What may have appeared to the audience as a couple lost in the rapture of the dance was really an intimidated girl and a man tugging and muttering, his strong stringy arms guiding her.

In the desert, a few miles before the Rocky Mountains, we paused for fuel at a desolate gas station and its small, nearly empty lunchroom. After the car's tank was filled, just before I turned the ignition key, a tall lean fellow emerged from the station and asked us for a ride to a mountain settlement where his wife was about to give birth to their first child.

Kay was sober that afternoon. We hadn't passed any roadhouses in miles. She looked him over and judged him trustworthy as he stood there, a petitioner, his cowboy hat in his big reddish hands.

He squeezed himself into the back of the car and we took off for the mountains. He was a cook in a nearby work camp, he told us, provided for by Roosevelt's National Recovery Act.

The road was rarely traveled then, a narrow blacktop clinging to the slopes and rises of the Rockies like a vein of coal. "Ma'am, can I drive?" he asked. I was glad to relinquish the wheel. It had grown dark, and he switched on the headlights. We passed no one.

He leaned over the steering wheel, his long-fingered hands gripping it. His hollowed-out cheeks and eyebrows, his whole face in the dashboard glow, looked old. I guessed he'd married a young woman. Now he was flying toward her like a devil, or an angel.

We arrived at a small settlement in the middle of a range of the mountains. It sent out a dim light among the trees like a weak flashlight. What looked like a small community center was a walk-in clinic, a single bulb hanging from its roughly carpentered porch roof. He stopped the car and, extricating his long legs and feet encased in cowboy boots, thanked us and said goodbye.

"What's happening?" asked Kay, who had fallen asleep. As I drove away from the settlement, I could see the tall cook in the rearview mirror, waving to us from the porch, and then he opened the door and disappeared. Soon there was nothing but the living darkness around us; our headlights seemed always on the point of being extinguished.

On the outskirts of Los Angeles, we stopped for the night at a large stucco house owned by a friend of Kay's and Kay's long-dead husband. Edwin came from a rich polo-playing family often in the newspapers; he had three ex-wives.

He was short and round, and his skin was the color of a mushroom. Although he was a contemporary of Kay's, he looked ancient, dried up. After Kay retired, he chased me around his patio for a few minutes. I suddenly stopped running and looked at him. He stopped too. I realized his mind was not on me; he was only following an inane ritual that he must have felt he owed to his reputation. I went into a bedroom off the patio. He followed, limping. We both lay down on the covers of the bed, and he fell asleep at once. For a person of his years, he had had a lot to drink that evening.

I slid away from him and walked down the corridor to another bedroom, where I undressed and got into the bed. When I awoke, hours later, a Mexican servant was staring at me from the door. I hesitated, then said to her, *Buenos días*. She heard my accent—someone had told me once that it was recognizably Antillean—and smiled warmly. For many years, I preferred the company of servants, finding comfort and acceptance among them.

We had a breakfast with Kay's friend before we left. He behaved with a foolish effort at dignity, never looking at me. But it was too much. Kay asked, as I drove away from the stucco house, what had gone on during the night.

Kay rented a house on Beechwood Drive, not far from where I had lived briefly years earlier. I didn't spend much time there either.

Every evening, she drank herself into insensibility after she had taken her little dog for his walk. One night she returned, her hair and clothes rumpled, a look of soused outrage on her face. She shouted to me that a man had bitten her on her left breast. "Well," she cried, "what do you think of that!"

"I don't know. How can I know anything at all?" I said, and burst into tears myself.

She sobered up as I broke down. Dank air was blowing through the window; rain was coming. For the first time, I glimpsed my whole life. What a sinkhole! I recalled good periods, good times, but they weighed little against the bad. What bleakness! What awful struggles just to stay afloat!

She poured me a drink and I gulped it down. Then another. At once I was fiery with liquor. I saw everything with such clarity. The scene I had made was the only way I could confide my bewilderment—and I'd got her attention for once.

But all that came to my mind was how I had not come to Uncle Elwood's defense when my mother's second husband had said, in a quarrelsome voice, "What kind of a name is that? Blooming Grove, for crissakes!" And when my father had asked after "Uncle Cornbeef." They had both been deep in their cups at the time. I saw liquor's benefit; it made everything come into the present. No time passed. Time stood still.

The next morning, I wrote a note to a Las Vegas gambling club I had heard of, asking for the job of "house shill." Several days later, I received a reply from the club owner. It said there were no openings, but from now on I would be wiser to call the position "house dealer" rather than "shill." That is, if I meant to write to other gambling clubs for work.

I had a brief disastrous marriage to an actor I had met at International House. He had come to California on a ship. He was part of the crew, what was called then an "able-bodied seaman"; it was his regular work. He was almost twice my age. He said we'd better get married, and I could think of no alternative, though I didn't like him very much.

I was underage, so I was obliged to get parental consent. It took me several days to find out where my father was living and write to him. He sent me a telegram that included his permission and the words "if that's what you want."

We were married by a judge in Los Angeles City Hall. By then he had found a cheap place to live on Hollywood Boulevard, at the very end before it went into a tunnel and emerged on the other side into the city.

The room, which came with kitchenette and bathroom, was skimpily furnished and gloomy. I knew nothing of domesticity. When he sent me out with a handful of bills, I went into a food shop and bought sausages in pastry, what the clerk who waited on me called "toads in blankets." He made a scene when I returned with them and asked me if I knew nothing. Of course I knew nothing.

I would have been one of those children found in a wilderness, written about in case histories, if it had not been for

Uncle Elwood; I had learned civility and kindness from him. I knew how to behave in parlous circumstances, to temporize and compromise, a lesson taught me by my father. From my mother I had gained the knowledge of how to contend with the madness of people. And from black servants, I had learned what justice was.

A few days later, after I had brought home the toads in blankets, I found a job as a waitress in a Greek café. The actor picked me up after I had worked there a week and we went into Los Angeles. I thought he was going to take me out to dinner. Instead, he took me to a bus terminal, where he boarded a bus bound for New York City.

He had saved that news for the last ten minutes. He was to join the crew of a merchant ship bound for Murmansk in the Soviet Union. He would be gone for months.

The thought of returning alone to that room was intolerable, but I played dead, like a possum. I stood by the looming bus, watching shadowy figures find seats through dusty windows. I couldn't see my new husband. It was as though he'd vanished.

I didn't have time to think much about the actor's abrupt departure. The restaurant where I worked was a meeting place for caddies from the golf courses around Hollywood and wanderers with movie ambitions from all the states in the union.

A redheaded man came in every day, headed for the

jukebox, put in a coin, and selected the same record, a Sibelius piece, *Finlandia*. He sat on a counter stool, listening to the music and making a somewhat theatrical display of his response.

I constructed hundreds of shrimp cocktails during the time I worked for Gus, the owner of the restaurant. During the days, I wasn't lonely. But at night in the furnished room, my solitariness spoke from the unmade bed, the rickety table, the small frying pan on a greasy burner, the few articles of clothing scattered about on the floor. In the closet hung the blue tweed suit I was still saving for a special occasion—of which there was none.

One evening I called Vincent Lawrence from a telephone in the corridor. I had found his number in a frayed phone book hanging by a chain. He told me to take a cab to Arizona Canyon, where he lived; he would take care of the fare. He was surprised to hear from me. He didn't know I had returned to California.

His house was large; a narrow brook ran through the grounds. It reminded me of the waterfall I had fallen into years before. The unlocked door opened to a wide hall and a circular staircase. The Lawrence family were at the dinner table. Vin smiled up at me as I stood hesitantly in the door to the dining room. Then he covered his face with a large linen napkin. As he spoke, his breath fluttered the cloth. It was his version of a scene.

Some members of his family were there, including his sister-in-law September, as he had nicknamed her. His wife, South, also renamed by him, and two of his three children were there; they kept their eyes on their plates. It was September who had irked him. Mild sarcasm, as I learned from my occasional visits to him over the years I spent in California, was the only expression of anger he permitted himself. That, and a certain eccentricity, as with the linen napkin hiding his face.

He abruptly rose and held out his hand to me. "Come on, pal. We're going upstairs to have a powwow."

I followed him to the stairs, up them, down a hall, into his bedroom, where he handed me two acts of a play he had written. I noticed holes in his blue sweater. "What do you think about it?" he asked, after I had read the neatly typed script. I had not been asked my opinion on anything since Balmville days.

I met an old actor from the silent screen when he came into the Greek restaurant. It was midafternoon. We got to talking. He worked in the wardrobe department of Warner Brothers studio now, and referred to himself as a *wardrobe mistress*. He had always wanted to be called mistress. When he was younger, he had longed for beautiful young men, but two had blackmailed him, he told me.

He called me *sister* and we planned to meet for supper at some other place. After we'd eaten, I was able to persuade him to stay in the room with me. We huddled together on the bed, two orphans of the storm, he observed.

I went on working for Gus until the actor-sailor-husband returned. As it turned out, he hadn't gone to Murmansk but to a safer, closer port. We moved into a small apartment on Ivar Street about to be vacated by another actor and his wife. They were old acquaintances of my husband's from the days of the Federal Theater, when they had worked in the cast of Marc Blitzstein's *The Cradle Will Rock*.

Before he left, a suitcase in either hand, the vacating actor grinned at me, remarking that the mattress of the bed had seen good service and was ready for more.

I flushed. Was the whole world grinning and fucking? Didn't sex need the privacy the actor had invaded? Wasn't an illusion of exclusivity the essence of sexual life? He might just as well have moved the seat of the toilet up and down, saying it was ready for more action.

I met other acquaintances of my husband's—some called themselves progressives, some were Communists. Equality for black people, an astonishing thought in those days, drew me to the Communists. I went to a fund-raiser for the party. It was given in a town on a lake. I met a black textile worker from the South. There was a moment when he and I stood on a deck and talked. He was shy and sweet-natured, I thought. I looked at his face and wondered if the scars on his cheek were from a beating he had undergone. But he said, No, it had been a car accident. He had been on a picket line, though, when his factory went on strike, and he had been beaten by the local sheriff.

One night my husband got drunk. At some moment during the evening, someone slipped a photograph under the front door, taken by a street photographer, of a woman I knew, holding my husband's arm. I showed it to him. He told me he was taking her to Palm Springs for a few days. I protested. He picked up a flimsy chair and broke it across my back. I fled into the dark. Where would I go?

Gus, the man for whom I had worked until recently, might still be in his restaurant. I found him standing behind the bar, cleaning up after the day's customers.

He hugged me and said I could spend the night at his apartment, where he lived with his ancient Greek mother. I slept on a couch. The next day I went back to Ivar Street. My husband was gone. There was a note from him on a table. *I'm taking a ship out of San Diego back to the East Coast. I'm spending a few days in Palm Springs before that.* It was signed, *With love.*

It was true that I was domestically undereducated, but I could get jobs.

I worked for a magician and was sent on an errand to deliver a book to Orson Welles, who would be at the Brown Derby. Armed with a purpose, I inquired of a man standing at the bottom of a curving flight of stairs in the restaurant where I might find Mr. Welles. He smiled and pointed up.

At the top of the stairs, a group of men made way for me, and at their center I saw Orson Welles, young and thin, smiling at me somberly, provocatively. I gave him the book and left.

I worked in a ceramic factory, where I painted sleeping Mexicans on pitchers and vases. Sombreros covered their faces and they leaned against giant cacti.

I taught dancing at Arthur Murray's until the place closed down for lack of customers. Everyone, I thought, knows how to dance in Hollywood.

I found a vile job in a storefront business where three fat men played craps all day long, rolling the dice on a desk pushed to a wall. Behind them, in another room, eight Mexican girls and I sat at bins sorting rivets the men collected weekly at airplane plants.

During the fifteen-minute break in the mornings, I remember how we gathered in front of the store, smoking cigarettes, and how the girl who had brought them crumpled the empty pack and said, "No more. We got to go back in."

We were paid by the weight of the rivets sorted out from dross.

I had heard about labor unions. I looked up the CIO in a telephone book and went to a local office.

I didn't know if there was a special way to speak with the

union official in whose glum office I sat. I told him about the dim bulbs over the bins, the breaks, even those for our lunch, which lasted only as long as it took to smoke a cigarette before we were summoned back by the three men, and last, the pay. I fell silent, my head filled with half thoughts: the official's face, his gray skin, his poker face, exploitation of workers. He rose to his feet and said, "We'll look into it."

I went back to the rivet store where, in order to take the morning off, I had pleaded illness. The pile in my bin was higher. The girls greeted me in Spanish, asked after my health, and said they were sorry I had been sick—they had missed me.

A few days later, when I arrived at seven in the morning, the store was closed up, and the three men and my fellow sorters were gone.

I rented a room in a house in a nondescript neighborhood, part of the Los Angeles sprawl already beginning then. An elderly woman and her embittered, divorced daughter with two young children owned it. I had a spacious, comfortable room. My wardrobe had increased to include a skirt, underwear, a pair of tennis shoes, and a cotton blouse. I still had the blue tweed suit that I had worn day after day in the LA dress shop.

Among the people I now knew was a Hungarian refugee who had set out to make her fortune designing clothes. She had rented an empty store on Hollywood Boulevard for an evening's show of her work. She asked me and another young woman to volunteer our services by modeling her fashions. She required Betty and me to cover our nipples with bits of adhesive and then dressed us in two of her many outfits, some of which still had basting thread on their seams.

Betty, who worked in a movie studio for a company run by Orson Welles, lived in a nearby apartment, so we went there during an hour's break in the show. She was elegant and slender, the first pretty "progressive" I had met.

As she unlocked her door, I glanced down the hall. Looking only at a key he was about to insert into the lock of another door was a familiar face and figure. Betty whispered to me, as we entered a big living room, that she was used to seeing him. He had a girlfriend in the building. It was Harpo Marx.

Daddy had told me he'd once had an office next to the Marx Brothers at some film studio. He'd heard them playing craps all day long instead of working on their scripts. The rattle of dice is like no other sound, he said, and it echoed through the cheap thin walls.

Late in the evening, after the showing of the Hungarian's line of clothing, I left. From down the street, I heard an actor's agent I knew slightly calling my name. I walked toward him, and the brightness from a large glass window of another storefront where an art show was being held. He invited me in.

As I entered, I spotted John Barrymore at once. He was yellowing with age like the ivory keys of a very old piano.

Maybe his drinking, as well as the years, had aged him too. He was sitting on a couch around which art lovers of the screen world were flowing in a constant stream, looking mostly at each other.

Barrymore was surrounded by four or five young women. I didn't give myself time to think—otherwise I wouldn't have done it—but walked directly to him, saying, "I bring you greetings from Kay M—." He looked up at me and waved the girls away.

He wanted to know how I'd met his old friend. I told him about driving to California with her, leaving out her drinking. He was kindly and quiet-voiced with me. After our brief conversation, he left with his bodyguard, a man who took care of him when he went on one of his drinking binges, I heard later. A short obese man called out, "Good night, sweet Prince." Barrymore gave him a dark look and turned in my direction. "Good night, lass," he said.

He reminded me of my father, not in his looks but in his voice and style and servitude to alcohol.

The post office sent me a notice that they were holding a package for me, LIVE GOODS, I think it said. I stopped by the local branch to pick it up. My father had sent me an infant alligator in a small crate. It was perhaps a foot in length.

I was so disappointed I nearly wept on the spot. But then a wave of laughter broke over me. It was the last thing I needed.

I named it Dolores and kept it in the backyard for a

few days. Members of the family I was living with came out to look at it every so often. I finally gave it to a supplier of animals to the movies who lived in the neighborhood.

One idle afternoon, I telephoned Republic Studios. I didn't call a second time, but they phoned me after a few weeks. I attributed it to movie perversity. By the time they called, I had gotten still another job reading South American novels for Warner Brothers, turning in triplicate reports written on a borrowed typewriter as to their film possibilities.

The paper quality of the books varied from country to country. I recall how thin and silky the Chilean pages were, yet not transparent. I was paid six dollars a book and given six or seven novels a week. It wasn't bad pay for those days.

One evening I went out with a Mexican girlfriend to a restaurant and nightclub. I danced for an hour or so with John Wayne, who was very young and handsome and thin and talked to me in a companionable way on the dance floor about the movies, or, as it was called, "the industry." He hadn't yet become a star but he was on his way. He liked all things Mexican: food, ambiance, women.

There was a party given in the neighborhood, to raise money for a Spanish refugee organization, in a house very like the one I lived in. We all went to it, the elderly woman, her divorced daughter, even the two children. I wore the blue tweed suit.

We could barely squeeze into the narrow hall, it was so crowded with people. In the living room, a group was gathered around two card tables upon which were soft drinks and a half-empty bottle of gin. A man with a small-featured intense face was holding forth in a voice that sounded like flowing gravel. He was smiling wryly, perhaps at himself.

Allen Adler was his name, and he told me he had a cleft palate, which I had guessed.

Would I go with him to the Garden of Allah and meet his cousin? He was so genial, nearly affectionate, I agreed at once. I didn't know what the Garden of Allah was or where it was or who his cousin was, but I wanted to hold on to the atmosphere, like a spotlight of energy, that he breathed.

The Garden of Allah turned out to be a collection of bungalows where noted people stayed, those who were only passing through Hollywood on their way to other better places, those who were waiting to take screen tests, and those on alcoholic binges. I suddenly recollected as we drove on our way that my father had said he had once stopped by there and left a five-dollar bill on a bureau in a bungalow rented by F. Scott Fitzgerald, who was lying on the bed nearly passed out. He had lifted his hand weakly as Daddy left.

A nimbus of illuminated dust made a halo around a tall lamp outside of a large bungalow. Inside, in the living room, was Allen's cousin, Stella Adler, her husband, Harold Clurman, a playwright, Clifford Odets, and a heavily made-up young blond woman named Carol, who, Allen whispered to me, must have fallen in love with her rouge pots. I sat down on a sofa next to Stella, who encouraged me by patting the seat cushion next to her with a smile that promised intimacy. She was refined and at the same time raffish, and her voice was full of depths and fluting melodies.

They all went back to the subject under discussion, which Allen and I had briefly interrupted, the marriage of Artie Shaw to Lana Turner. Shaw was urging books upon her, lecturing her, hectoring her. Stella held up her pretty hands. "He wants to educate her against her own wishes. What a darling situation!" Then she turned toward me. "*Educate* her," she murmured in an amused, confiding tone.

I was nearly fainting with self-consciousness in such company, and excited by it, sweating in my tweed suit and not only because of the weather. Stella got up and went into another room. When she returned, she was holding a large photograph of a painting of a dark-haired child.

"My daughter, Ellen," she said wistfully. I loved Stella at that moment, and I thought to myself that Ellen was the most fortunate of children, the inheritor of every marvelous thing, especially the velvet dress she was wearing in her portrait.

Then she rose again. When she came back this time, she was carrying a blue covert-cloth suit in her arms as though it were an infant.

"May I give you this?" she asked me.

Everyone in the room had fallen silent. Odets hit a piano key softly, middle C.

"I think it's the right size," she said.

Harold Clurman nodded his head and smiled at me. Allen said *hurrah*, for no apparent reason. I took the suit.

Elsie and Linda

When Elsie was ninety-two, dying of old age and emphysema, two of my three children urged me to visit her on the island of Nantucket, where, as far as I knew, she had been living for more than three decades. I had not seen her for thirty-eight years.

I wanted to please them. I had no desire to see her. With my permission, my daughter had given her my telephone number. She called me. I heard the old seductive voice, deep and familiar as my own. I felt the same harrowing tension for a moment; then it went, and it was as if I were speaking politely to an utter stranger.

I went to the airport the next day, but Nantucket was fogged in and the flight was canceled. I hardly had the nerve for a second try. But I made it without the nerve. I landed on Nantucket around noon. I took a taxi to her address; the driver was a voluble old bohemian who had lived on the island since the late sixties.

Her house was one of several like it in a new community

extending out from the port town. As I got out of the car, I thought of my grandmother, dead and buried without my having been told. "She wouldn't have been interested," Elsie had said of me, one of my uncles reported. Perhaps I had deserved it. But not from the woman who was my mother. I looked at the house and shuddered. The door was unlocked.

I walked into a conventionally furnished living room. From a small room on the left came a sound that I told myself, grimly, was a minotaur breathing, but it was only an oxygen-supplying machine. I looked inside. My mother was asleep on a big bed. I averted my eyes from the figure beneath the bedclothes.

I must have sat in the living room for twenty-five or so minutes, looking at a magazine I had found on a table, when I was aware that someone was looking at me.

I put the magazine down. My mother was standing a few feet away, swaying slightly. She reminded me of an old conquistador, thin, tall, white hair like a helmet. I would have recognized her anywhere.

"Paula?" she asked, beginning to smile.

"Yes," I answered, as I stood up. She was wearing a thin white cotton nightgown. Her chest bones protruded slightly. Her skin was transparent and tinged with a bluish cast.

We shook hands. I followed her into her bedroom just as the front door opened and a young couple entered. They were her caretakers, a South American Indian from Peru and his plump young American wife, pale, with frizzy dyed-blonde hair. They lived in a spare room upstairs.

He addressed my mother as señora. They had been out on an errand. He was a trained nurse. While I sat in a chair next to her bed, he brought her a drink that looked like malted milk. With a winsome smile, she commanded him never to leave her. Then, still smiling, she asked me if he didn't have a "perfect Indian head." I thought of Francisco Pizzarro cutting off such heads.

I detected panic behind her effort to keep him charmed, an infant's fear of the dark.

She asked me to go to a room across from hers and bring her a photograph. I went, found a closed door, opened it, and saw the floor was covered with boxes filled with papers. On the top of one box was a sepia-colored photograph of a man standing in front of a horse and carriage in parkland. I brought it to her.

"Who do you think this is?" she asked archly.

I shrugged. She answered her own question dramatically. "Your grandfather! And the horse? It was his own, sent him from Cuba to New York City. Her name was Beauty. He said American horses were too slow for him."

She laughed and then had to use the oxygen machine. I put her drink down on a table. She had barely touched it.

"I want you to have this photograph," she gasped. She stopped speaking, and the nurse came into the room.

I went out, and when I came back she had played her trick; she had hidden the picture under the bedclothes knowing, somehow, that I wouldn't want to search there for it. I didn't ask her where it was, although I couldn't help casting glances at the bed.

I needed to urinate. I excused myself and went outside and walked until I found a field and a tree. I couldn't use a toilet Elsie might have used. My revulsion was so deep, I took the chance that someone might spot me crouching next to the tree trunk.

I don't know what we spoke about during the hours I spent with her. At some point, I mentioned my brothers and sister and their mother, Mary, and she held up her hand.

"I still can't hear her name," she said. I knew it had been over half a century since she had spoken to Mary. When my father died and I had called to tell her, she had made polite uninterested noises.

I went to the airport an hour earlier than I needed to, hitching a ride with the nurse who, as we drove off, told me he had a part-time job: standing on the small Nantucket airfield holding two lighted rods to guide the incoming airplanes.

He parked in front of a small airport restaurant I had been too tense to notice when I landed that day. It was dark now, and patches of light from the windows glowed on the ground.

I walked inside. There were tables, a counter with a plastic cake stand, a coffee machine, a waitress wearing a short black skirt beneath her apron, and an open window to the kitchen. The customers were few: a family with two children, a young middle-aged couple, two men holding hands, a man in a business suit reading a newspaper, two young women speaking earnestly to each other. I sat down at a table, its surface gritty with grains of sugar.

I was surrounded by the saints of ordinary life, and for an instant I felt that God was in the restaurant. After Elsie.

A few months later, the nurse's wife telephoned me at home to say Elsie had died that morning. I murmured something comforting and realized I had spoken as if Elsie's death was the wife's loss.

When I hung up, I felt hollow, listless. I had lost out on a daughter's last privilege; I couldn't mourn my mother.

When I was two weeks away from my twenty-first birthday, I gave birth to a daughter. During my pregnancy, I had gone to an agency for financial help, Native Sons of California. A beefy-faced man looked at my swelling belly and said, pointing to a bench, "Sit down, dear. You'll have a long wait."

After a while, I got up and left. My labor lasted a day and a night. In the San Francisco hospital where I went for my confinement, babies were brought into the ward in their wheeled cribs. From the corridor just outside, two nurses looked in at me. I heard one of them say, "Not her."

I must have been on a low floor, because I could see, through a window near my bed, the branch of a tree, leaves, a small bird. All the women around me nursed their infants. I had put my daughter up for adoption.

Ten days later, I went to see one of the doctors who had

been an intermediary in the adoption and asked for her back. The doctor told me it was legally too late. I didn't know any better, so I accepted his lie as truth. I had asked a second doctor who was involved in the adoption to find a Jewish family to take her. I guess to comfort me, he said jovially, "He travels fastest who travels alone." The world is filled with empty phrases. He hadn't even gotten the gender right, and he didn't get the family right. They were middle-aged Sicilians.

Many years later, Linda found me. One Saturday I received a thick FedEx envelope. I was sitting in my kitchen when I opened it. There was a handwritten note on the top of a letter, and it said, "Go slow."

I knew at once. I called up the stairs to my husband, "She's found me."

We wrote every day for three months, sometimes twice a day, telling, telling, telling.

We didn't speak on the telephone during that time. We both understood that our communication was to be written. She suggested we meet somewhere, perhaps Santa Fe, New Mexico, where, if we got bored with each other, there would be other sights to see.

I suggested San Francisco, where we had been parted. She agreed. Her assistant telephoned me to make arrangements, and I flew there one day in mid-May.

When the airplane was a few hundred yards from the ground, I wished it would crash. In the face of great change, one has no conscience.

It was eleven-thirty and a clear day in San Francisco. I walked off the plane and into the airport waiting room. I hadn't gone more than a few feet when I heard running steps behind me. I turned to look at the woman who was doing the running. We both laughed at the same time. We walked so closely together, I could feel her breath on my face.

"Have you got a cigarette?" she asked me. "I quit yesterday," she added.

I gave her one. "Let's go in there," I suggested, pointing to an airport bar we were about to pass.

We spent two hours drinking soda, talking. I found her beautiful. She was the first woman related to me I could speak to freely.

I have had splendid close friendships with women, beginning with Bernice in elementary school. What I had missed all the years of my life, up to the time when Linda and I met, was freedom of a certain kind: to speak without fear to a woman in my family.

We went to a hotel where we spent four days together, most of the time in the hotel, like lovers. We had separate rooms and we left notes under each other's doors. She told me she had wondered about who I was all her life. She had guessed I might be Marilyn Monroe, or a murderous old woman she had seen once on a bus.

We spent one of the days in what felt like an eternal traffic jam, headed toward Carmel. When silence fell between us, there was no tension.

She asked me again about her father—she'd written me that question.

I told her that the day her first letter had reached me I had called him up in Los Angeles, where he had lived for many years. His widow informed me that he had died a few months earlier. What did I want with him? the widow asked. I was an old friend, I said. I had yielded to him once one evening, rather gracelessly.

Linda and I went to the street where I had lived when I had been pregnant. I had rented a room on Telegraph Hill in a two-story building that was the only house left there from the forties.

We sat on the curb and looked up at two dark windows. I told Linda how a black friend had carried me to the bathroom the first day I had come home from the hospital, after she had been born.

I'll leave us there, sitting close together on the curb. Now and then someone passed by but paid no attention to us as we told each other stories from our lives, falling silent every so often.